The Gospel of Anger

Also by Alastair V. Campbell
from SPCK:

MODERATED LOVE
A Theology of Professional Care
(1984)

PAID TO CARE?
The Limits of Professionalism in Pastoral Care
(1985)

THE GOSPEL OF ANGER

Alastair V. Campbell

First published in Great Britain 1986
SPCK
Holy Trinity Church
Marylebone Road
London NW1 4DU

Second impression 1989

British Library Cataloguing in Publication Data

Campbell, Alastair V.
    The gospel of anger.
    1. Anger—Religious aspects—Christianity
    I. Title
    248.4   BV4627.A5

ISBN 0-281-04221-7

Photoset and printed in Great Britain by
WBC Print Ltd, Bristol

Contents

Acknowledgements   vii

Preface   ix

1 God of Anger – God of Love   1

2 The Lethal Link: Anger and Destructive Aggression   17

3 Lover or Demon? The Wrath of God in the Bible   33

4 The Prison of Hostility   50

5 Anger and Liberation   66

6 The Fire of Love   82

Notes   108

Index   116

Acknowledgements

V. Axline: Extract from *Dibs: In Search of Self* reproduced by permission of Victor Gollancz Ltd and Houghton Mifflin Co. Inc.

James K. Baxter: Lines from 'Jerusalem Sonnets' from the *Collected Poems* reproduced by permission of Mrs J. C. Baxter.

T. S. Eliot: Lines from 'Little Gidding' from the *Collected Poems 1909–1962* reprinted by permission of Faber and Faber Ltd and Harcourt Brace Jovanovich Inc.

Robert Frost: Lines from 'Fire and Ice' from the *Complete Poems* reproduced by permission of Holt, Rinehart & Winston.

G. Guareschi: Extract from *Don Camillo's Dilemma* reproduced by permission of Farrer, Straus & Giroux Inc.

R. D. Laing: Extract from *The Politics of Experience and the Bird of Paradise* reproduced by permission of Penguin Books Ltd.

Louis MacNeice: Lines from 'Brother Fire' from *The Collected Poems of Louis MacNeice* reproduced by permission of Faber and Faber Ltd.

James Matthews and Gladys Thomas: Lines from *Cry Rage!* reproduced by permission of Spro-Cas Publications.

Ogden Nash: Lines from 'Visitors Laugh at Locksmiths or Hospital Doors Haven't Got Locks Anyhow' from *Verses from 1929 on* reproduced by permission of Little, Brown and Company and Curtis Brown Associates, Inc. copyright 1940 by The Curtis Publishing Company.

Wilfred Owen: Lines from 'Soldier's Dream' and 'The Last Laugh' from *The Complete Poems and Fragments of Wilfred Owen* volume 1, edited by Jon Stallworthy, reproduced by permission of the author's estate and Chatto & Windus.

Siegfried Sassoon: Lines from 'Stand To: Good Friday Morning' from *Selected Poems* reproduced by permission of George Thorneycroft Sassoon, executor and Viking Penguin Inc.

Ian Crichton Smith: Lines from 'Old Woman' from *Selected Poems* reproduced by permission of Victor Gollancz Ltd.

Stevie Smith: Lines from 'Anger's Freeing Power' from *The Collected*

Preface

This book has been in preparation – perhaps 'simmering' would be the right word! – for the past four years. I was first able to use the privilege of a sabbatical term in 1981 to work through the basic literature in theology and psychology and to draft out some preliminary ideas (subsequently published by The Westminster Pastoral Foundation[1] and by the *Modern Churchman*[2]). At that time my colleagues thought it their duty to keep interrupting my sabbatical peace with trivial inquiries in order to keep my anger level up! To their credit, this was *not* successfully achieved and at the conclusion of an intellectually restorative break from teaching I felt that I must consign much undeveloped material to an academic 'freezer', until opportunity came to work on it again.

That opportunity did come in the shape of an invitation to deliver the Thomas Burns Memorial Lectures in the University of Otago. The lectures were delivered there in the spring of 1985 but, in addition, a selection from them was delivered in two other academic centres in New Zealand – Auckland and Christchurch.

The stimulus of preparing these public lectures, plus the lively audience participation and response in all three centres, has been invaluable to me in ordering, clarifying and extending my thoughts on this complex subject. Since returning from New Zealand I have carried out another substantial revision and expansion of the material in preparation for publication. No doubt many deficiencies remain, but I feel sure that the book is a better one (and I hope a more useful one) as a result of the challenges and creative interchanges I was offered by many friends and colleagues in New Zealand.

I also owe a debt of gratitude to my many colleagues here in Britain. In a subject with so many interdisciplinary aspects the list is inevitably a long one, but perhaps for that reason also, worth giving. For points of detail in theology, biblical studies, pastoral implications, psychology and psychiatry I have consulted George Anderson, Graeme Auld, Kay Carmichael, Duncan Forrester, John Gibson, Peter Hayman, Murray Leishman, Alan Lewis, David Lyall, Ian McDonald, Andrew Ross, Douglas and Elizabeth Templeton, and Henry Walton. I am also indebted to Judith Longman of SPCK who saw the pastoral weaknesses of the first draft and encouraged me to write in a manner closer to the everyday situations of anger which the reader might encounter. Elma Webster has once again worked tirelessly on my manuscript, helping not just with typing but with her own reactions to what I was writing. My wife Sally claims that she has the greatest part in the preparation, as the main instigator of my anger! But, for my part, I know that without her love, support and stimulus I would not have persevered in finding the positive side of an emotion which I, like many others, find it hard to express and to accept. I hope this book will be of help to those who see the title as both a challenge and a threat.

Edinburgh, November 1985   Alastair V. Campbell

ONE

God of Anger – God of Love

Yet each man kills the thing he loves
By each let this be heard
. . . . .
The coward does it with a kiss
The brave man with a sword.

Oscar Wilde, 'The Ballad of Reading Gaol'[1]

It is a fearful thing to fall into the hands of the living God.

Hebrews 10.31 (AV)

We are familiar – perhaps too familiar – with the idea that the Christian gospel is the good news of love and that our response to this gospel should be to love God and our neighbours as ourselves. But could Christianity also be a gospel of anger? And could being angry with our neighbours and with God also be a part of the Christian life? These ideas sound strange, but, as we shall see, anger and love are not as far apart as we might at first imagine, and in pastoral situations anger can be a potent influence for good. Yet finding the positive side of anger is not an easy task, especially since traditionally it is associated with punishment and revenge. The anger of a loving God is an enigma which requires some solution; and human anger has undeniably a destructive and personally damaging aspect. We must, therefore, begin our quest for anger as good news by examining the apparent conflict between the love of God and the anger of God. This will prepare the way for a full exploration of the nature of human anger.

THE ENIGMA OF THE 'ANGRY' GOD

In the Order for the Visitation of the Sick contained within

Cranmer's *Book of Common Prayer* (1549) the priest is
instructed to inform the ill person that 'whatsoever your
sickness is, know certainly that it is God's visitation', for,
'whom the Lord loveth he chasteneth and scourgeth every son
whom he receiveth'. We find a similar approach in the
Westminster Directory of the Public Worship of God (1645).
The sufferer is exhorted 'to make a sanctified use of God's
visitation, neither despising his chastening nor waxing weary
of his correction'. Such a robust approach to suffering seems
alien indeed to those who offer pastoral care in this modern
age. Schooled as we are in the virtues of empathy, non-
possessive warmth and unconditional acceptance we cannot
serve easily the punishing God of the Puritan divines. On the
contrary, when faced with a person in irremediable suffering,
we are far more likely to encourage them to express *their* anger,
including their anger at God, than to exhort them to humble
submission to God's chastening rod.

This, then, is the enigma of the angry God which is nowhere
more powerfully felt than in the field of pastoral theology.
How can we reconcile the idea of a God who cares for us as
tenderly as our own father and mother, who rushes to embrace
us as we return from the far country, who loves us so much
that even his own son is sacrificed for our sakes, with the stern
and punitive God who deliberately causes us pain and sorrow?
Where is the unconditional and restorative love of God if he
can act so cruelly against us? As we think of this we hear the cry
of the despairing Job, the man who lost everything that was
dear to him *because* of his loyalty to God:

> In anger God tears me limb from limb . . .
> I was living in peace,
> but God took me by the throat
> and battered me and crushed me.
> God uses me for target-practice . . .
> he attacks like a soldier gone mad
>   with hate.
>   Job 16.9, 12, 14 (TEV)

The bitterness which Job feels can be stronger still if we
witness the seemingly senseless suffering of another person
whom we are powerless to help. In *The Bird of Paradise* R. D.
Laing recounts this profoundly disturbing case study of a little

boy whose simple request goes unheeded and whose pain seems beyond any theological justification:

> He was ten years of age and had hydrocephalus due to an inoperable tumour the size of a very small pea, just at the right place to stop his cerebrospinal fluid getting out of his head, which is to say that he had water on the brain, that was bursting his head, so that the brain was becoming stretched out into a thinning rim, and his skull bones likewise. He was in excruciating and unremitting pain.
>
> One of my jobs was to put a long needle into this ever-increasing fluid to let it out. I had to do this twice a day, and the so-clear fluid that was killing him would leap out at me from his massive ten-year-old head, rising in a brief column to several feet, sometimes hitting my face.
>
> Cases like this are usually less distressing than they might be, because they are heavily doped, they partially lose their faculties, sometimes an operation helps. He had had several, but the new canal that was made didn't work.
>
> The condition can sometimes be stabilized at the level of being a chronic vegetable for indefinite years – so that the person finally does not seem to suffer. (Do not despair, the soul dies even before the body.)
>
> But this little boy unmistakably endured agony. He would quietly cry in pain. If he would only have shrieked or complained . . . And he knew he was going to die.
>
> He had started reading *The Pickwick Papers*. The one thing he asked God for, he told me, was that he be allowed to finish this book before he died.
>
> He died before it was half-finished.[2]

Yet, when we consider the anger of God, especially as it is portrayed in parts of the Old Testament, we have not yet encountered the worst, even in this case. There is an awesome destructiveness in Jahweh, which seems to go far beyond anything which could be regarded as fatherly chastening or a test of faith of individuals. Consider the terrible warlord in Isaiah 63 (celebrated in an image which reappears in the New Testament Apocalypse (Rev. 19.15)):

> I have trampled the nations like grapes . . .
> I trampled them in my anger, and their blood
> has stained all my clothing.
>
> Isa. 63.3 (TEV)

How often do congregations realize as they lustily sing the
Battle Hymn of the Republic ('Mine eyes have seen the glory of
the coming of the Lord'), that the God they celebrate kills
without mercy?:

> I, and I alone, am God;
> no other god is real.
> I kill and I give life, I wound and I heal,
> and no one can oppose what I do . . .
> I will take revenge on my enemies
> and punish those who hate me.
> My arrows will drip with their blood,
> and my sword will kill all who oppose me.
> I will spare no one who fights against me;
> even the wounded and prisoners will die.
> Deut. 33.39, 41b–42 (TEV)

There is worse still to come when we consider other aspects
of the Lord's anger in the Old Testament. For in places he
appears to be quite wilfully destructive, a sinister and irrational
force which seeks people out in order to victimize them. Two
notable incidents are the census reported in 2 Samuel 24 and
the circumcision of Moses' son in Exodus 4. In the former
incident Gods tells David to carry out a census of Israel in order
to 'bring trouble on them' (2 Sam. 24.1). Seventy thousand
Israelites die as a punishment from God for the census which
God himself ordered. In the latter incident God visits Moses,
'and tries to kill him' (Exod. 4.24), the death being averted
only by a ritual circumcision of his son by his wife Zipporah.
We read elsewhere of a God who deliberately prevents people
from repenting so that they may be punished as a sign of his
lordship (Exod. 10.1–2), and who so preserves his holiness
that any incursion into it (even accidental) brings instant
destruction (Exod. 19.20–2; 1 Sam. 6.19; 2 Sam. 6.7–8).

There is no escape from the enigma of the angry God when
we consider all these dimensions of his nature, especially those
portrayed in the earlier parts of the Old Testament. Christian
theologians have been obliged to seek some explanation that
will preserve the nature of God as a God of love. At the risk of
oversimplification we may identify three types of solution to
the enigma: (1) Some aspects of the biblical portrayal of God's

anger are rejected as primitive and unacceptable to a proper understanding of the Christian gospel; (2) The anger of God is related to his holiness, a mysterious aspect of his nature which is in tension with his love; (3) The anger of God is seen as part of the passionate seeking for human wellbeing which characterizes his love. I shall discuss each of these explanations quite briefly at this stage, since a full exploration will require a careful explanation of both the biblical material and insights about the nature of anger derived from modern sociological and psychological theory. The function of this brief survey will be to set an agenda for the subsequent discussion, and to lead us on to the second concern of this opening chapter, the place of human anger in the context of a gospel of love.

A Savage God?

If some portrayals of the anger of God seem to contradict his love then the simplest solution is to discard the incompatible elements. This is the approach taken by C. H. Dodd in a celebrated passage in his commentary on Romans: 'In the long run', he wrote, 'we cannot think with full consistency of God in terms of the highest ideals of personality and yet attribute to Him the irrational passion of anger.'[3] Dodd therefore discards 'the simple anthropomorphic idea that God is angry with men',[4] in favour of what he regards as the developed New Testament view that 'wrath' or 'the wrath' is an impersonal force, 'an inevitable process of cause and effect in a moral universe'.[5] This approach has been elaborated and defended in a very scholarly fashion by A. T. Hanson in his book, *The Wrath of the Lamb*. After surveying the concept of divine anger from the varieties of description in the Old Testament, through the inter-testamental literature to the range of New Testament materials culminating in Revelation, Hanson argues that the concept has been purged both of its irrational elements and its anthropomorphic reference. He concludes: 'the wrath of God is the punishment of God, and the punishment of God is what he permits us to inflict on ourselves, God . . . *permits wrath*, but he is love.'[6]

The solution offered by Hanson finds expression in a hymn by John Keble, which describes the Old Testament God using new methods when, as witnessed in the New Testament, he reveals a very different nature:

> When God of old came down from heaven
> In power and wrath he came
> Before His feet the clouds were riven
> Half darkness and half flame
>
> But when He came the second time
> He came in power and love;
> Softer then gale at morning prime
> Hovered his holy Dove.[7]

Keble concludes his hymn with the request, 'Save, Lord, by love or fear'. We shall see in the next sections the theological critique to be offered to this solution, but first it will be interesting to notice commentary from another quarter. In *Answer to Job* C. G. Jung argued that one cannot discard the dark side of God. The relationship between love and Jahweh's 'rage and jealousy' was to be regarded not as an irreconcilable split in his nature, but as a necessary antimony. According to Jung, 'God is not only to be loved, but also to be feared. He fills us with evil as well as good.'[8] To ignore the dark side is to ignore both the complexity of human nature and the mysterious nature of God. In *Our Savage God* R. C. Zaehner pursues the same line of argument. A God of revelation must be a terrible God, for otherwise we end up with a dualism which puts evil outside the control of God, Thus, Zaehner concludes (in an echo of the lines from Oscar Wilde at the head of this chapter): 'God certainly kills the things he loves, but the things he loves rejoice to be killed at such a hand.'[9]

These ideas from Jung and Zaehner offer a direct challenge to the rationalizing of the theologians. In effect, they argue that the rationalist's God is no God at all, that far from being a primitive concept to be discarded, the modern world cannot dispense with a savage God. This is a crucial issue, which will reappear in many forms as we view anger from different disciplinary perspectives.

A Holy God?

A second major way of resolving the enigma of God's anger is to see it as a reflection of his holiness. As Karl Barth puts it: 'There is the purity, indeed He is Himself the purity, which as such contradicts and will resist everything which is unlike itself . . .'[10] The view is to be distinguished from Dodd's and Hanson's explanations because it purports to explain all aspects of God's anger and because it regards it not as an impersonal force but as an integral feature of God's relationship to humankind. Thus Barth emphasizes the reciprocal connection of judgement and grace: 'God is holy because His grace judges and His judgment is gracious'.[11] In light of this, Barth can assert that to distinguish the living relationship of grace from a 'heathen quietism' we must realize that 'To accept God's grace necessarily means . . . to respect God's holiness, and therefore to accept, heed and keep His laws, to fear His threats, to experience His wrath and to suffer His punishment.'[12] Yet, in harmony with his dialectical approach, Barth constantly reiterates that, despite this judgement, wrath and punishment, we know in the same experience the redemption from the consequences of our sinfulness wrought by Jesus Christ. Thus Barth, unlike Luther and many subsequent Protestant theologians, will make no separation between the revelation of the wrath of God and the revelation of his grace.

The difficulty which Barth leaves us with is that his account appears to cancel out (albeit in a more subtle way than the simple rejection of the 'primitive' by Dodd and Hanson) the more fearsome aspects of the anger of God portrayed in the Bible. Holiness in Barth is morally explicable, and ultimately redemptive, holiness. It is hard to see how it can encompass the Lord who rides on the wings of the storm, coming as a consuming fire to those who have provoked his wrath (Isa. 66.15; Jer. 23.19).

Other writers have not hesitated to use the concept of God's holiness as an explanation for his destructive wrath. So Leon Morris: 'a holy God wills to pour out the vials of His wrath upon those who commit sin'.[13] Morris believes that there are both deeds of wrath and deeds of mercy and in both God is personally active. So also in R. V. G. Tasker's *The Biblical Doctrine of the Wrath of God* we have a separation of divine mercy and divine anger. Tasker sees the revelation of the full power of the wrath of God as a prerequisite for grace: 'To

realise that we are under God's wrath and in dis-grace is the
essential preliminary to the experience of His love and His
grace. In this respect the Christian gospel is bad news before it
is good news.'[14]

Such views allow the writers to accept with considerable
equanimity the highly destructive activities of God when
confronted by his enemies or by the apostasy of his chosen
people.[15] They both deny, however, that God's anger is way-
ward, spasmodic or unpredictable. Tasker describes it as 'stable,
unswerving, and of set purpose'. [16] Morris argues that it is not
'some irrational passion bursting forth uncontrollably, but a
burning zeal for the right coupled with a perfect hatred for
everything that is evil'.[17] Neither writer offers an explanation
for the more bizarre episodes of divine anger referred to earlier
in this chapter. It is difficult to see what sin Moses had
committed the night the Lord attacked him, or how Uzzah
could be blamed for stumbling and touching the ark (2 Sam.
6.7–8). Indeed, unless 'holiness' is to be understood as
containing an element of mystery not accountable in moral
categories, it is difficult to see how the explanations of Barth,
Tasker and Morris account for the total picture of God's anger
given in the Bible. Perhaps (less obviously than Dodd and
others) they have an edited or at least reinterpreted version of
the Bible according to their understanding of revelation.

A Passionate God?

In the accounts surveyed so far a solution to the enigma has
been sought by defining God's nature in a way which
encompasses (and perhaps justifies) his anger. But what if we
have a God 'who reacts in an intimate and subjective manner'?
(A. H. Heschel)[18] In such an approach the traditional
impassivity of God has to be abandoned for a more dynamic
and (probably thereby) less coherent view. Instead of rejecting
the ascription of passion to God, as anthropomorphic and
thereby blasphemous, some theologians regard it as the only
way of speaking of the living and incarnate God of Christianity.
As Rosemary Haughton observes in *The Passionate God*:
'Love . . . is experienced not only as peaceful creativeness but
as violent breakthrough';[19] and according to Heschel the Bible

finds the source of evil 'not in passion, in the throbbing heart, but rather in hardness of heart, in callousness and insensitivity'.[20]

With such an explanation of God's pathos we enter the violent world of Donne's religious sonnets:

> Batter my heart, three personed God; for, you
> As yet but knocke, breathe, shine and seek to mend;
> That I may rise, and stand, overthrow me, and bend
> Your face, to break, blow, burn and make me new
> . . . for I
> Except you enthrall me, never shall be free
> Nor chaste except you ravish me.[21]

Here it is the zeal of God to recapture the beloved which gives a dangerous fire to love. 'The secret of God's anger is God's care'[22] and the fearfulness in falling into the hands of the living God (Heb. 10.31) derives from the power of his love alone. In *The Crucified God* Jürgen Moltmann has developed this idea in terms of the suffering, the pathos, of the covenant God:

> What the Old Testament terms the *wrath of God*. . . [belongs] in the category of the divine *pathos*. His wrath is injured love and therefore a mode of his reaction to men. Love is the source and the basis of the possibility of the wrath of God. The opposite of love is not wrath, but indifference . . . As injured love, the wrath of God is not something that is inflicted, but a divine suffering of evil. It is a sorrow which goes through his opened heart. He suffers in his passion for his people.[23]

The attractiveness of this third type of solution is that it seeks to hold on to the centrality of love in God's relationship with humankind, but at the same time does not deny the reality of God's anger. As we shall see later, this account of the interpenetration of love and anger may be closer to the ordinary human experience of love than the polarity of love and anger implied by the previous two accounts. Moltmann is surely right that the opposite of love is indifference, not anger. Yet, once again, perhaps this explanation is too tidy. Will the language of covenant, typical of the prophetic literature, cover all that might be said about the anger of God? There appear to be many loose ends. As Jim Garrison points out in *The Darkness of God: Theology after Hiroshima*, it is hard to explain the excessive destruction in God's actions or to justify his deliberate hardening of the hearts of those who oppose the covenant people. Thus, while sympathetic to the idea that we gain deep insight into the anger of God by seeing him as the crucified one, Garrison is troubled by the surplus destructiveness and 'display of raw anger' in much of the biblical material. He therefore concludes:

> Vengeance and repentance alone do not suffice to explain the wrath of God. There is something deeper going on within the Godhead itself, something that defies conventional morality or even covenantal promises. It suggests a certain intention on the part of Jahweh to give vent to a dark side of the Divine even as Jahweh gives vent to a lighter side.[24]

Thus we return again to a mystery in God's anger, a mystery well described by Rudolph Otto as *tremendum et fascinans*. Where that mystery will lead us is yet to be seen, but it is clear that no one explanation can contain all that might be said about a God of love who is also an angry God.

HUMAN, ALL TOO HUMAN

So far I have written as though the only problem which confronts the pastoral theology of anger is the seeming incompatibility in the nature of God. But an equal, if not greater, problem faces us when we consider what, in the light of all this, we are to make of human anger. Is divine anger justified but human anger always to be deplored? Or are they both in that category of 'irrational passion', which Dodd thought must be transcended? Alternatively, are there occasions when both human anger and divine anger can be viewed as creative forces in the service of love? Let us consider one of the many incidents of anger described in the delightful Don Camillo stories of G. Guareschi:

> [Peppone, the Communist mayor, has come to the church to 'bump off that cursed priest' for a sermon condemning 'the Reds'. Through a window he sees Don Camillo hammering at the supporting column of the pulpit.]
> 'Father, are you pulling the church down?'
> Don Camillo looked up with a start and in the light of the candle burning before the statue of Saint Anthony he saw the face of Peppone.

'Not I,' he answered. 'Other people make that their business, as well you know. But it's no use. The foundation is solid.'

'I wouldn't be sure of that,' said Peppone. 'Solid as it may be, it isn't enough to protect the deceivers who hide behind it in order to insult honest men.'

'Quite right,' Don Camillo replied. 'There's no salvation for the deceivers who insult honest men. Only here there's no such deceivers.'

'You're here, aren't you?' Peppone shouted. 'And you're a hundred deceivers rolled into one.'

Don Camillo clenched his teeth and kept his self-control. But once Peppone had started, there was no limit to what he would say.

'You're a coward and a liar!' he shouted.

Don Camillo could contain himself no longer, and hurled the hammer at the chapel window. His aim was terrifyingly exact, but God willed that a gust of wind should cause a hanging lamp to swing in such a way as to deflect the hammer from its course and send it into the wall, a foot from its destination. Peppone disappeared, leaving Don Camillo in the pulpit, with his nerves strained to the breaking-point. Finally he shook himself and went to confide in the crucified Christ over the main altar.

'Lord,' he said breathlessly, 'did You see that?' 'He provoked and insulted me. It wasn't my fault.'

Christ made no answer.

'Lord,' Don Camillo continued. 'He insulted me right here in the church.'

Still Christ was silent . . .

'It's late,' Don Camillo reflected. And he added: 'But it's never too soon for an act of humility.'

He walked rapidly through the darkness. Most of the village houses had gone to sleep but there was still a light in the workshop of Peppone. Don Camillo groped for the catch of the iron grille. The shutters were open and he could hear Peppone breathe heavily as he hammered out a red-hot iron bar.

'I'm sorry,' said Don Camillo.

Peppone stared, but quickly took hold of himself and continued to hammer without lifting his head.

'You took me by surprise,' Don Camillo went on. 'I was nervous . . . When I realised what I had done, the hammer was already out of my hands.'

'You must be slow-witted, Father, if you don't wake up to your misdeeds until after you've committed them.'

'There's some merit in admitting a mistake,' said Don Camillo cautiously. 'That's the sign of an honest man. When a man won't admit that he was wrong, than he's dishonest.'

Peppone was still angry and went on pounding the iron, which had by now lost its red glow.

'Are we going to begin all over?'

'No,' said Don Camillo. 'I came to put an end to it. That's why I began by asking you to excuse the unforgivable gesture I made against you.'

'You're still a coward and a liar. And I'll put all those hypocritical excuses of yours right here!' And Peppone slapped the base of his spine.

'Quite right!' said Don Camillo. 'That's where stupid fellows like you keep everything sacred.'

Peppone couldn't stomach it, and the hammer flew out of his hand. It was aimed with diabolical accuracy at Don Camillo's head, but God willed that it strike one of the narrow bars of the grille. The bar was bent, and the hammer fell on to the workshop floor. Don Camillo stared in amazement at the bent bar and as soon as he could move, he set off at full speed for home and arrived, all choked up, at the foot of the altar.

'Lord,' he said, kneeling before the crucified Christ, 'now we're even; a hammer for a hammer.'

'One stupidity plus another stupidity makes two stupidities,' Christ answered.[25]

The story of Don Camillo, in constant yet affectionate battle with the Communist mayor and with his Lord, suggests that anger may have a positive as well as a negative side. The association with humour is not an accidental one. Like humour, anger can often reflect the human capacity to transcend the immediate situation, gain a new perspective and effect a change for the better – or, if that is not possible, at least register a protest at the wrongness of that which cannot be changed. Moreover, anger is most usually sparked by the friction of personal encounters and its intensity can reflect the important place which some other people occupy in our lives. Thus Don Camillo's combative relationship with Christ and with Peppone suggest a closeness which (in the latter case) he might well deny. Don Camillo's irascible nature is loveable because we see where his loyalties lie and what he really cares about beyond the confines of conventional religion. Thus there can be an honesty in anger, an openness which reveals the human face rather than the masks of social conformity. This half irritated, half humorous relationship with a puzzling God, who seems at times to ask more than is reasonable from fallible humans, is equally well captured by the Jewish writer Sholom Aleichem in his stories about Tevye the Milkman (now popularized in the musical, *Fiddler on the Roof*). The following, for example, is Tevye's reaction when he discovers the luxury in which some Jews live:

'Gevalt, Gottenyu,' I thought. 'They say you're a long-suffering God, a great God; they say that you're merciful and fair. Perhaps you could explain to me why it is that some folk have everything and others have nothing twice over? Why does one Jew get to eat butter rolls while another gets to eat dirt?' . . . A minute later, though, I said to myself: 'Ach, what a fool you are, Tevye, I swear! Do you really think He needs your advice on how to run the world? If this is how things are, it's how they were meant to be; the proof is that if they were meant to be different, they would be.'[26]

Thus Tevye, by tussling with God, comes to an answer which satisfies him just as Don Camillo gets from Christ a devastating response to his sense of self-righteous wrath. But human anger is not always so amusing or so positive in its effects. Like the anger of God, it has its dark side. Giving vent to angry feelings is rarely itself a solution to either personal or social problems. Often it sours relationships and creates situations of conflict which cannot be solved without a loss of face by one or other party. We can be amused by the quarrels between Don Camillo and the mayor, but we know that in the real world, as well as in the little world of Don Camillo, the fighting priest's methods usually make matters worse, and violence escalates. In Tevye's world, too, the resignation of the poor Jew will not be the 'final solution'. Ahead lies victimization of rich and poor alike and violence against Jews in Russia and throughout Europe. So there is a bitter irony in Tevye's resentment and in his dreams of being rich and happy. Too often the outcome of anger is human destructiveness of terrifying proportions.

Thus alongside the ambiguity of the divine wrath we must place our uncertainty about the origins, function and moral value of human anger. Martin Luther said of it, 'Anger refreshes all my blood, sharpens my mind, and drives away temptations . . . perhaps in this way God is revealing the fictions of men. For I see that that which is treated quietly in this age soon passes into oblivion.'[27] As we shall see later, there is much good common sense in this statement. It describes what in modern psychological terms is categorized as the 'state of arousal' which anger represents, and it shows that anger can be a positive force for change. On the other hand, Luther ignores the potentially destructive effect of anger, however 'righteous'. But then Luther never did pay much heed to the epistle of James ('that epistle of straw'), where he would have heard some contrary advice: 'Let every man be quick to hear, slow to speak, slow to anger, for the anger of man does not work the righteousness of God' (Jas. 1.19 RSV).

PROSPECT

Where, then, do we go from here? Is the notion of an angry God really compatible with that of a loving God? Is human anger always to be deplored or can it sometimes have positive effects, both on our relationships with fellow humans and on our relationship with God? These are not merely theoretical questions, of concern only to psychologists and theologians. Anger is woven into the fabric of our daily lives and (as we shall see in chapter four) its effects on human health and wellbeing can be devastating. Yet to be without anger may well lead to the 'oblivion' which Luther describes, where nothing changes and where eventually love itself loses all power. There is perhaps no more crucial pastoral question than that of the use, or abuse, of anger. Pastors must frequently deal with angry people and, because of the uncertainly they feel about their own angry feelings, they usually find themselves out of their depth. The 'gospel of niceness' has had such an effect on Christian groups that anger is constantly evaded, denied and thereby exacerbated. Christians feel uneasy with an angry God – and with their angry selves – and so, like children seeing ghosts in bedtime shadows, their fear of that which they only half understand and are too frightened to look at grows and grows. Faced by injustice, the contempt of others, the affront of death or just the petty frustrations of living with others, those who fear and deny anger experience a gnawing guilt which drives them deeper into themselves and further away from the true causes of their anger.

It is imperative, then, to seek as much clarity as possible in this crucial area of human relationships and religious belief. The task will not be an easy one, because, as must already be evident, the subject is a complex one. There is no shortage of practically-minded books telling Christians how to deal creatively with their anger.[28] But (in my judgement) these books all evade the really difficult issues by an over-simplification which fails to see the inherent ambiguity in both human and divine anger. In this book I tread a more difficult path: in the next two chapters I shall seek to look squarely at the 'dark shadows' which haunt us in our perceptions of our own and God's anger. Chapter two confronts the painful reality of human destructiveness (human beings are the greatest killers of all), and seeks to set anger in a physiological and psychological context which will explain its potential for both creativity and violence. In chapter three, I shall return to the enigma of the angry God, exploring the many different biblical images used to portray divine wrath. The outcome of this exploration will be to find a God who is closer to us, more involved with us, than we might at first think. But yet a mystery remains and the elusive God, the God difficult to trust, will continue with us to the conclusion of the book, when the central question of pastoral theology will be asked: How do we learn to live with God? As stages on the way to this final question, I shall be returning to the place of anger in human life, looking first at its power to injure and destroy (chapter four) and then at its power to liberate in both personal and socio-political contexts (chapter five).

The path ahead is a tortuous, but not (I hope) a tedious one. This is a journey full of surprises, as unexpected views are revealed when the road twists and turns. Luther was right that anger 'refreshes the blood'. Life is rarely dull when anger is close by, and, though at times we may be filled with dismay at the seeming callousness of humans and of God, the hot blood of anger can also reveal a richness of character in that which, until now, we had seen much too complacently and without imagination. Perhaps some paradoxical verses of the devout but ever-questioning George Herbert will be the best foretaste of the trip ahead. The title of his poem, 'Bitter-Sweet', is a good summary of what we must experience if we want to know the reality of anger, human or divine:

> Ah my dear angry Lord,
> Since thou dost love, yet strike;
> Cast down, yet help afford;
> Sure I will do the like.
>
> I will complain, yet praise;
> I will bewail, approve;
> And all my sour-sweet days
> I will lament, and love.[29]

TWO

The Lethal Link:
Anger and Destructive Aggression

The eyes gleam, the countenance trembles, the tongue
stammers, the teeth chatter, the visage is alternately
stained now with redness spread over it, now with white
paleness.

Lactantius[1]

Man is the only mammal who is large-scale killer and
sadist.

Erich Fromm[2]

> Throw away thy rod:
> Though man frailties hath,
>   Thou art God:
> Throw away thy wrath.

George Herbert,
'Discipline'[3]

My concern in this chapter will be with the possible link
between the powerful emotional reaction of anger and acts of
destructive aggression against the instigators of that reaction.
Is that link a necessary one, or is it possible to express one's
anger by more creative methods? We must first understand the
nature of the bodily state we interpret as 'anger', and then
survey various theories intended to account for the markedly
aggressive features of human behaviour. I shall be arguing that,
in human anger, perception, interpretation and choice of
actions permits an uncoupling of the link between feelings of
anger and aggressive acts. Human beings are potentially the
most destructive of all animals, especially in relation to their
own species, but they are not *necessarily* so.

THE PHYSIOLOGY OF ANGER

Lactantius' vivid description of the bodily manifestations of anger, quoted above, shows that from ancient times anger has been well understood as associated with a physiological reaction. The common Hebrew words for anger or being angry, *'aph* and *'anaph*, refer to the nostril and thus to snorting with emotion, while *chemah* ('to be hot') depicts anger as a kind of burning. These ideas are combined in Psalm 18.8 (TEV):

> Smoke poured out of his nostrils,
> a consuming flame and burning coals
> from his mouth.

The Septuagint and the New Testament use two words: *orgē* a thrusting or upsurging, and *thumos*, a boiling up. (In the New Testament *thumos* generally refers to human emotional reaction, whilst *orgē* is reserved for the 'breaking out' of the wrath of God in punishment.) The English word 'anger', derives from the Latin root *ang* – a narrowing, thus referring to the choking sensation associated with rising emotion. The aptness of these words is evident from more scientific accounts of anger in mammals:

> When anger is aroused in mammals, there is an increase in pulse rate and blood pressure, together with an increase in the peripheral circulation of the blood, and a rise in the level of blood glucose. The rate of breathing is accelerated and the muscles of the limbs and trunk become more tensely contracted and less liable to fatigue. At the same time, blood is directed from the internal organs of the body, and digestion and the movements of the intestine cease, although the flow of acid and the digestive juice tends to be increased . . . During anger there is also a diminution of sensory perception – so that men who are fighting can sustain quite severe injuries without being aware of them.[4]

It can be seen from this description that a good general description of anger would be 'arousal'. (Moreover, the associated circulating and digestive effects are important, as we shall see later (chapter four) when we consider the effect of anger on health.) According to the researches of the physiologist Cannon there exists a 'fight/flight' mechanism, a response to threat of the sympathetic nervous system. A rush of adrenaline brings about the bodily changes described above, preparing the body to react to the danger either by fighting or fleeing. This discovery reveals why it is that fear and anger have such similar bodily effects. Research since Cannon has sought to discriminate between them in terms of differences in biochemical triggers. The normative study was that of Albert Ax, who discovered the presence of a second hormone, noradrenaline, in angry subjects. (The same subjects in situations of fear secreted only adrenaline). But more careful investigation suggests that all that Ax discovered were differences in intensity of arousal, which are then interpreted by the research subjects as fear or anger, according to the situation in which they find themselves.

In human subjects surges of adrenaline and noradrenaline provide 'the *feeling* of a feeling' and the higher the circulating levels the more we are likely to feel overwhelmed by emotion. But the physiological reaction is not itself the specific emotion. Rather, human beings learn to interpret the arousal as a specific emotion, according to their perception of the situation, itself influenced by cultural factors and by individual differences in attitude. This point is summarized by Carol Tavris as follows:

> If anger shares the physiological symptoms of joy, excitement, fear, anxiety, jealousy, and the like, it means that anger is not the inevitable consequence of arousal but an acquired one. It means that anger is generated and reduced by how we interpret the world and the events that happen to us.[5]

This conclusion is of vital importance for the question of the connection between anger and our aggressive acts. For, if in humans there is no biologically conditioned 'fighting instinct' but only a state of arousal which is open to diverse interpretation, then human anger is much more malleable than a simple biological determinism would imply. What then is the origin of human aggression? To seek to explain what Anthony Storr has spoken of as 'the sombre fact that we are the cruellest and most ruthless species that has ever walked the earth'[6] becomes a major priority for anyone who also seeks some positive value in human anger. Is Tennyson right when, contrasting with his often quoted lines about nature 'red in tooth and claw', he sees

'Man, her last work, who seemed so fair', as the worst monster?

> A monster then, a dream,
> A discord. Dragons of the prime,
>   That tare each other in their slime,
> Were mellow music matched with him.[7]

What is the explanation for the destructiveness which under-mines humanity's claim to be a 'higher' species?

HOMO HOMINI LUPUS

In *Civilisation and its Discontents*, Sigmund Freud wrote of the inevitability of an 'aggressive instinct' in human beings:

> men are not gentle, friendly creatures wishing for love, who simply defend themselves if they are attacked . . . a powerful measure of desire for aggression has to be reckoned as part of their instinctual endowment . . . *Homo homini lupus*; who has the courage to dispute it in the face of all the evidence in his own life and in history?[8]

Yet the assertion that 'man is wolf to man' *would* be disputed, partly by the observation that the predatory behaviour of wolves and other animals pales into insignificance beside the wholesale destructiveness of which humans are capable; and partly by questioning whether, in any case, comparisons with animal behaviour are in any way illuminating when we consider the complexity of human aggressive acts.

The Instinct Theory

Konrad Lorenz is the most celebrated exponent of the view that intraspecific aggression is a necessary component of animal behaviour, including the behaviour of human animals. Lorenz sees aggression as a 'spontaneous instinct', resulting from the build-up of energy within an individual organism, a build-up which must find some release. (This has been called the 'hydraulic' view of instinctual drives, and it has close similarities with Freud's early instinct theory.[9]) The exercise of aggression is, Lorenz argues, necessary for the survival of the species. It services territoriality, the spacing out of the species over the available habitat; it ensures that the better specimens are successful in obtaining mates; and it aids social organization through the establishment of a rank order. At the same time the species-endangering aspects of pent-up aggressiveness are controlled through elaborate rituals (whether it be the triumph ceremony of the greylag goose or the parliamentary and courtroom rituals of humans), whose purpose is to check the aggressive drive 'without really weakening it or hindering its species-preserving function'.[10] Lorenz accepts that human aggression has got out of hand to the point where it is in danger of destroying the species, but his evolutionary approach lacks an adequate explanation of how this has come about, or how it can be circumvented. Thus one is left wondering whether the comparison with intraspecific aggressive behaviour in animals is at all helpful. Human aggression appears to be in a different class and to be in need of an explanation which describes specifically human motivation.

Freudian Formulations

In the formulations of Sigmund Freud we have a similar assertion that aggression is biologically innate, but a rather more complex set of explanations. Freud offered three different theories of the origins of aggression, corresponding to the development of his general theory of instincts: (1) His first theory is similar to Lorenz's in that he saw aggression as an aspect of the basic life force he named the Life Instinct. This consisted of the instinct to self-preservation and the instinct to preservation of the species (libido or sexual instinct). So powerful was the sexual drive that it provoked murderous and incestuous wishes, revealed in the Oedipus Complex. (2) Freud, however, was to modify this view substantially when he recognized the need of the rational part of the personality (the ego) to regulate the 'blind striving' of the instincts in order to adjust to the realities of the outside world. This 'instinctual renunciation' resulted in the transformation of libido into aggression, either in the form of self-punishment (guilt) or in the form of hostility towards others. (3) Finally, in *Beyond the Pleasure Principle*, Freud postulated a third theory which introduced a new concept, the Death Instinct or Thanatos.

There was, Freud believed, in all living things 'an urge to return to the quiescence of the inorganic world',[11] expressing itself in an innate destructiveness which was locked in perpetual conflict with the urge to survival. Thus, according to Freud, 'the aim of all life is death'.[12] Human aggression is not at all surprising. It shows merely the pervasiveness and power of the death instinct, which in the end will always have its way.

Of these three theories the second has been the most influential, since it seems to offer a testable hypothesis, in contrast with the seeming mythologies of the Oedipus Complex and of Thanatos. The idea that aggression is the product of frustration found a detailed formulation in the work of Dollard *et al.*,[13] who set about testing the correlation without resort to a Freudian theory of instincts. The importance of this formulation is that it implies that aggression is a product of social interaction, not an instinctive and inevitable drive. Were it possible to show what forms of frustration lead to the most serious forms of aggression, then it would be theoretically possible to reorganize human society in such a way that the causes of aggression were, if not eliminated, at least reduced to a minimum. Unfortunately, the frustration-aggression hypothesis has a number of problems.[14] Firstly, frustration does not appear to be the only instigator of aggression. As Cannon suggested in his postulation of a 'fight/flight' mechanism, the physiological arousal evoked by threat can also lead to the priming of aggressive behaviour. Secondly, aggression can be a learned response to situations in which there is no prior frustration or threat. For example, an individual or a nation can discover that aggression is effective in increasing their wealth or their power over others and, if offered no effective counter-threat, may become increasingly aggressive in pursuit of their aims. Thirdly, the concept of frustration is itself unclear, since what is regarded as an unwarranted restriction on behaviour by one individual may be regarded by another as a reasonable constraint to be accepted without violent reaction. Thus, as we saw with anger in humans, so also with frustration: no single factor seems adequate to account for the complexity of the behaviour, and the specifically human contribution of inter-pretation of events appears at least as important as any predisposing biological or psychological 'causes'.

Benign and Malignant Aggression

Such complexity has led Erich Fromm, in his extensive study, *The Anatomy of Human Destructiveness*, to offer a classification of aggression into different types, each of which requires a separate explanation. Fromm identifies the fundamental problem to be that 'only man appears to be destructive beyond the aim of defence or of attaining what he needs'.[15]

This 'hyper-aggression' in man Fromm calls 'malignant aggression' and he distinguishes it from 'benign aggression', which is biologically adaptive and life-serving: Fromm sees the latter as defensive, a response to threat or to the frustration of basic needs, and necessary for human survival. This is not to say that he sees no problem in benign aggression, but the solution to it lies in alleviating the adverse conditions which make it necessary, e.g. overcrowding, shortage or maldistribution of resources, or the stressful conditions of modern life. Benign aggression can be a creative force leading to social change and to a more humane society. But malignant aggression is another matter. Fromm describes it as follows:

> [it] is not a defence against a threat, it is not phylogenetically programmed, it is characteristic only of man; it is biologically harmful because it is socially disruptive; its main manifestations – killing and cruelty – are pleasureful without needing any other purpose; it is harmful not only to the person who is attacked but also to the attacker. Malignant aggression, though not a human instinct, is a human potential rooted in the very conditions of human existence.[16]

The most frightening aspect of this form of aggression is that it does not follow from that bodily arousal we call anger. It may itself bring about arousal of some kind (sexual or quasi-sexual), as in the phenomenon of sadism, but its origins are more obscure than the threat which provokes anger. It is chilling and deadly destructive because it is 'cold' rather than 'hot'. In a short poem, Robert Frost captures the point in the images of fire and ice:

> Some say the world will end in fire
> Some say in ice.
> From what I've tasted of desire

I hold with those who favour fire
But if I had to perish twice
I think I know enough of hate
To say that for destruction ice
Is also great
And would suffice.[17]

Thus in malignant aggression we encounter those phenomena which led Freud to postulate a 'death instinct', a primitive urge for lifelessness, quiescence. Fromm, however, offers a quite different theory. It is, he believes, the denial of the specifically human, the frustration of existential needs, which creates senseless destructiveness. He traces malignant aggression to a spiritual malaise in modern life, the loss of a sense of rootedness in society and the loss of a sense of unity within self and with nature. From this there develops the terrible *ennui* of post-industrial society, which is related to a loss of any feeling of purpose or even of usefulness in one's life. These features of modern life, when combined with specific personal life histories which mould character, lead to two coldly violent solutions – that of the sadist, who feels pleasure in the infliction of pain and the humiliation of others; and that of the necrophiliac, who has a 'passionate attraction to all that is dead, decayed, putrid, sickly . . . the passion to tear apart living structures'.[18] Using as his case illustrations Stalin, Himmler and Hitler, Fromm tries to show how the conditions of modern life have the potential to create psychic cripples, of whom these historical figures are only the extreme examples. Only when we have a society which allows us to *be*, not merely to *have*, to develop our creativity, imagination and co-operativeness with others, will we have any hope of ridding ourselves of malignant aggression. The problem is a spiritual one, not merely a question of sociopolitical change.

ANGER, AGGRESSION AND HATRED

Fromm's ideas are clearly of the greatest interest to anyone concerned to understand the relationship between anger and destructively aggressive acts. It is obvious that anger does lead to violence. The arousal created by threats or frustrations prepares the body for actions of a physically aggressive type.

Indeed the connection is often so close that we speak of 'blind rage' as the cause of injury to others or of wanton destruction of property. But such a view is an oversimplification of the link between anger and acts of aggression. It omits an essential aspect of human behaviour – the contribution of cognition.

Imagine a situation in which you are hurrying through a crowded city street. Suddenly you feel a violent blow from somebody's fist on your right shoulder. Angrily you turn to remonstrate with the aggressor. (It is unlikely, unless you are a very short tempered person, that you would be prepared to be physically violent immediately.) Then you recognize your 'attacker' as an old friend you have not seen for many months. In an instant, your feelings change from anger to pleasant surprise and you greet your friend in return (perhaps also with a punch on the shoulder!). This incident illustrates the important cognitive links which can lead from anger to aggression – or in quite another direction – according to our interpretation and evaluation of the situation. So-called 'blind rage' is not an isolated phenomenon (except in those whose perception is affected by brain damage or by drugs). It represents the culmination of a series of acts which have been regarded by the enraged person as increasingly provocative or unendurably threatening. The outburst of violence, once the background is understood, can be given an explanation in terms of the aggressor's understanding of himslf or herself in that particular situation. It is not genuinely 'blind'.

We may clarify this important issue further by drawing a distinction between feelings of anger and the emotion of anger.[19] Immediate responses to frustration or threat are characterized by those bodily changes already described, which we experience as 'feeling angry' (or, alternatively, 'feeling afraid'). But the emotion of anger is a state of mind of a more complex nature in which we have associated those feelings with various perceptions, thoughts and (perhaps) fantasies. We recognize ourselves as being in a mental state of anger, and we usually already have, or are actively seeking, an explanation for it. Thus the emotion of anger entails what might be called a confirming interpretation (e.g. 'Yes, that remark by my colleague was rather insulting – no wonder I feel angry'). In the transition from feeling to emotion, which may be rapid or may

take some time, there is room for additional interpretation and
for choice. ('Am I being too sensitive? Perhaps I should check it
out with someone else. I certainly feel angry, but the insult may
have been unintended. In any case, what should I do about it? I
don't want a slanging match – or do I?') Thus we confirm, or
modify, our mental state and we consider possible courses of
action, including retaliatory ones.[20]

These complexities in the link between anger and aggressive
responses demonstrate the fallacy of confusing the arousal we
call 'feeling angry' with a supposed 'aggressive instinct'. It is a
matter of considerable debate (as we have seen above) whether
any human aggressive acts are instinctive in the normal
meaning of the term. What may be instinctive is a physiological
response to frustration or threat. The actions which follow
that response can be aggressive or non-aggressive according to
factors at least partly within the control of the individual who
is feeling angry. Moreover, the aggressive behaviour which
does follow anger is much more explicable and potentially
modifiable than those truly puzzling and frightening human
aggressive acts which are carried out 'in cold blood', as we say.
The 'malignant aggression' described by Fromm could well be
less malignant if we could get behind its senseless destructiveness
to that symptom of human vulnerability we call 'anger'. On the
basis of a considerable volume of research, the psychologist,
Buss, summarizes the following relationship between aggression
and anger: 'When aggression occurs in the absence of anger,
there is an increase in the tendency to aggress. When
aggression occurs in the presence of anger there is a cathartic
effect, i.e. a decrease in the tendency to aggress.'[21]

Repeated aggressive acts in the absence of anger develop
easily into a habit of violence with a decreasing sensitivity to
the personal implications of the attack on others.[22] The prime
example of this tendency is the 'war mentality' which spreads
rapidly in a population which would normally be tolerant of
those people now described as 'the enemy'. Certainly war also
entails major threat and enemy actions provoke anger mixed
with fear. But in order for the war effort to be sustained it is
necessary to generate hatred of the enemy, by depersonalizing
them (with nicknames like, 'Huns', 'Jerries', 'Japs', 'Argies')
and creating an attitude of hostility which will bridge the gaps

between the stimulation of anger by war casualties, fear of air attack, etc. It is such phenomena which may explain the cold atrocities of war, including the wholesale destruction of non-combatant civilians of all ages. It is not anger, but hatred, which is the true enemy of human peaceful coexistence.

WHAT TO DO WITH ANGER

It should be clear by this stage that there can be no single answer to the question, Should anger be expressed or controlled? There is no psychic force called 'anger', operating like an energy source in a machine. To be angry is to react in a human way, combining in a remarkably complex, yet unnoticed manner, signals from the external world and those interpretations necessary for perception with further interpretations of our physiological responses to that perception. Moreover, the awareness, 'I am angry' is not itself an instigator of any one action. It may prompt to aggression, but it does not cause aggression in a mechanistic sense. Even in extreme anger we are usually left with the decision to act aggressively or to refrain from action of a destructive kind. Thus the power of anger, for good or ill, is a power wielded by human agents and its use is a matter of human choice and responsibility. Later in this book (chapters four and five) I shall be examining ways in which anger can be detrimental to, or creative of, better human relationships. But for the present, I wish to dispose of two common oversimplifications, which I have called respectively, 'the ventilationist' fallacy and the 'bottle it up for God' fallacy. The latter (as is obvious in my description) is the more common mistake of religiously-minded people, but the former is perhaps now in danger of becoming a new (and equally misleading) 'gospel'.

'Letting Off Steam'

If, as the quotation from Buss given above indicates, the expression of anger has a cathartic effect, then it is tempting to suppose that by 'ventilating' our anger (giving full expression to it whenever we feel it) we can reduce the 'head of steam', as it were, and so avoid damage to self or others by a dangerous

build-up of violent feelings. The ventilationist philosophy
argues, in the words of Janov the founder of Primal Therapy,
'Make anger real and it will disappear.'[23] But, of course, human
beings are not steam engines and so the analogy, although
helpful in some situations (in particular when people have
inhibitions about expressing their feelings) eventually breaks
down. In normal human interaction, there is evidence to
suggest that for many people the experience of 'giving vent to
anger' can be so stimulating that it creates the desire for more.[24]
(We recall that the physiology of anger and of other intense
emotions, such as excitement or joy, is not dissimilar.)
Moreover, the experience of being angry always entails an
interpretation of bodily responses. Thus telling people to
'ventilate' their anger is encouraging them to label every
response to threat or frustration as anger, whether that is in
fact the interpretation they themselves would have applied in
the situation. Carol Tavris recounts a conversation overheard
in a café, between an apostle of the ventilationist school and a
friend whose own interpretation of her emotions was quite
different!

Woman A: You'll feel better if you get your anger out.

Woman B: Anger? Why am I angry?

Woman A: Because he left you, that's why.

Woman B: Left me? What are you talking about? He died. He
was an old man.

Woman A: Yes, but to your unconscious it's no different from
abandonment. Underneath, you are blaming him for
not keeping his obligation to you to protect you
forever.

Woman B: That might have been true if I were ten years old,
Margaret, but I'm forty-two, we both knew he was
dying, and we had time to make our peace. I don't feel
angry, I feel sad. I miss him. He was a darling father to
me.

Woman A: Why are you so defensive? Why are you denying your
true feelings? Why are you afraid of therapy?

Woman B: Margaret, you are driving me crazy. I don't feel angry,
dammit!

Woman A (Smiling):
So why are you shouting?[25]

Thus 'Woman A' proves her hypothesis, but only by means of creating the anger she is determined to find. The fallacy in ventilationism is that feelings (or attributed feelings) are given such priority over other aspects of human awareness, such as reflection and exercise of self-control, that quite unrealistic expectations are attached to the expression of feeling as a route to wholeness. Given the history of Western culture and given the powerful inhibitions associated with Christianity, it is understandable that there should be such a swing toward emotional catharsis and especially the release of negative emotions. But human wellbeing seems to depend more upon a balance of different aspects of the personality rather than upon an over-emphasis on any single aspect. Thus a failure to place anger in the context of the individual's own self-understanding and own moral values and choices results in as great a disregard of the person as the most extreme and unfeeling rationalism. Simply expressing anger when we feel threatened or frustrated is not an answer in itself.

Bottle It Up For God?

This is not to say, however, that the expression of anger is always to be deplored and avoided. A second oversimplification is the one more common in church circles and in the mainstream Christian tradition. This regards anger as an unworthy passion to be controlled at all costs. Reference is usually made to Jesus' saying in Matthew that anger and murder are to be equated,[26] or to the text from James 1.20 that 'the anger of man does not work the righteousness of God' (RSV). But, of course, a 'battle of the texts' easily ensues at this point, with the anger of Jesus and the prescription 'Be angry but do not sin' of Ephesians 4.26 (RSV) as ammunition for the defence. It seems easier to avoid such scriptural literalism and merely to point to the over-simplifications in the 'bottling-up' approach. Firstly, it ignores the reality of the bodily arousal associated with anger. We shall see later how destructive of physical and emotional health the denial of anger can be and how the fear of anger makes these destructive effects worse. To acknowledge that we feel angry is not the same as to give free reign to feelings which could damage our personal relationships.

The over-simplification and inappropriate moralization of the 'bottling-up' approach fails to see this difference. Secondly, to deplore anger as unworthy of Christians is to fail to see its close affinity to love. Beverly Harrison may overstate the point when she writes that 'Anger is a *mode of connectedness* to others and it is always a *vivid form of caring*.'[27] Anger can be many different things, of which caring is only one, but it still remains true that the opposite of love is not anger, but either hatred or indifference. Thus to banish anger entirely from personal relationships is to refuse to accept the degree to which one is vulnerable to others and so in a position to challenge them in the name of love to take notice of us.

The moral theologian, Bernard Häring, has a dramatic description of an incident of anger during his war-time experience as a German Catholic priest compelled to work as a medical orderly in Hitler's army. Significantly, Häring entitles the chapter in which the incident is described, 'Not Quite Like Christ'. (As we shall see in the next chapter, however, that lack of similarity could well be denied.)

> Near the end of the war, when the city of Danzig was already occupied by the Russians, we were in a large forest behind the city. The doctor and I were ministering to a number of wounded soldiers when a colonel came along, raging against the 'cowards' who would not fight.
>
> Realizing that he was one of the chief judges who had sentenced hundreds of good German soldiers to death because they saw no sense in the unreasonable prolongation of a lost war – or, in some cases, only because they had become 'displaced persons', lost from their units – I completely lost my temper. I turned on him, shouted at him, calling him a criminal and whatever else came to mind. The doctor and the soldiers around me stood aghast, their faces white, thinking that I would be the next one to hang. However, the colonel himself turned pale when he saw my fury, and disappeared.
>
> I am sure that he would have taken quick revenge if he had not realized the terrible revenge the men would have taken on him if he took any drastic steps against me at that moment. But I am still amazed that I got away unscathed after such an outburst.[28]

It seems appropriate to describe Häring's forthright expression of his anger both as a 'vivid form of caring' and as an example of quite remarkable courage. It demonstrates that it is always an oversimplification to put a single moral label on the expression of anger as unreservedly good or unreservedly bad. Instead the following balanced evaluation by Carol Tavris seems closest to the truth:

> Anger, like love, is a moral emotion. I have watched people use anger, in the name of emotional liberation, to erode affection and trust, whittle away their spirits in bitterness and revenge, diminish their dignity in years of spiteful hatred. And I watch with admiration those who use anger to probe for truth, who challenge and change the complacent injustices of life.[29]

SEVERING THE LINK

The task then which faces us, if the Christian commitment to compassion and to justice is to be honoured in the way we act towards others, as individuals and as nations, is to sever the link between anger and destructiveness and to find ways in which people's powerful reactions to life's dangers around them may be put to the service of human wholeness. These are fine sentiments, but in the real world the forces of human destructive aggression are so apparently invincible that the hope for an anger which creates rather than destroys love must seem a forlorn one indeed. Much more commonly anger seems to lead to an enduring hostility and to a hatred which finds satisfaction only in revenge. Moreover there is a fear which is even worse for Christians to face: there is the possibility that *even in God* the link between anger and destructive aggression cannot be severed. What hope then for human love, if that is so? The God portrayed in the Bible is far from unambiguous in the renouncing of revenge. Perhaps for some of us (for most of us?) his anger at our unworthiness makes us vessels fit only for destruction (Rom. 9.22). This terrible God, the shadow behind the God who loves us, we shall consider in the next chapter. The fearsome conclusion of W. B. Yeats' poem of a disintegrating world gives us a glimpse of that unwelcome spectre:

> Surely some revelation is at hand;
> Surely the Second Coming is at hand.
> The Second Coming! Hardly are those words out
> When a vast image out of *Spiritus Mundi*

Troubles my sight; somewhere in sands of the desert
A shape with lion body and the head of a man,
A gaze blank and pitiless as the sun,
Is moving its slow thighs, while all about it
Reel shadows of the indignant desert birds.
The darkness drops again; but now I know
That twenty centuries of stony sleep
Were vexed to nightmare by a rocking cradle,
And what rough beast, its hour come round at last,
Slouches towards Bethlehem to be born?[30]

Can love prevail against such dark forces? In constructing a pastoral *theology* of anger, we must seek answers to this basic question of faith in a loving God.

THREE

Lover or Demon?
The Wrath of God in the Bible

But ah, but O thou terrible, why wouldst thou rude on me
Thy wring-world right foot rock? lay a lionlimb against me?
  scan
With darksome devouring eyes my bruised bones? and fan,
O in turns of tempest, me heaped there; me frantic to avoid thee
  and flee?

Gerard Manley Hopkins, 'Carrion Comfort'[1]

> Love shall tread out the baleful fire of anger
> And in its ashes plant the tree of peace.

John Whittleaf Whittier, 'O brother man'[2]

The quest for an anger which serves love strikes a major obstacle when we consider honestly (and without a selectivity which favours our theological presuppositions) the pictures of God's wrath[3] which appear throughout the Bible. The material is rich and exceedingly diverse. In the Old Testament there are over four hundred references to the anger of God, occurring in literature of many different types, from early parts of the Pentateuch to late wisdom literature and apocalyptic writings. The New Testment provides a further twenty-nine references scattered across the gospels, the epistles and the Johannine Apocalypse. In addition there are less frequent, but nonetheless significant references to human anger, often in relation to God or to the religious life (eighty references in the Old Testament; eight (plus parallels) in the New Testament, two of which refer to the anger of Jesus).

As we saw in chapter one, some theologians seek a Marcionite solution to this diversity, simply ignoring those references which do not accord with their understanding of

Christianity. (This seems to be the solution favoured by most books dealing with pastoral aspects of anger. They 'tactfully' omit reference to the fearsome God of fire and storm.) Other theologians have attempted to offer a coherent interpretation of the diversity, usually by means of describing a tension between God's holiness and God's love. I do not regard either of these solutions as adequate, believing that we will gain a deeper understanding of the nature of anger if we try to come to terms with all the biblical themes – those which seem alien and frightening as well as those which seem familiar and reassuring. This does not commit us to a biblical literalism, but it does require that we take the whole of the Bible seriously, as a record of the struggles of faith over many centuries.

But if a single theological explanation cannot do justice to this diversity, it would be equally unhelpful, not to say tedious, to attempt to comment on every occurrence throughout the Bible. As an alternative I have chosen to group the material into six main themes, each portraying a certain image of the origin of divine (and, by analogy, human) anger. These themes are linked by the notion of power, but the character of power alters radically as the themes change, with a decreasing destructiveness and an increasing creativity. The first three themes – God as 'demon', 'tempter' and 'avenger' – are primarily negative, the 'dark side' of anger; the second three – God as 'lover', 'servant', 'saviour' – are primarily positive, the 'light side' of anger. But this dichotomy between positive and negative, dark and light, will prove to be too simple as we look at the full complexity of the picture which emerges. Especially it must be stressed from the outset that not all the 'darkness' is to be found in the Old Testament and not all the 'light' in the New. Rather we find an alternation of sunlight and shadow, and the stronger the sun the deeper the shadow. In the anger of Jesus in particular, the man for us, the man with us, the revelation of God's love, we find some of the deepest mystery.

THE DARK SIDE OF ANGER

The morally and theologically troublesome passages dealing with God's anger may be grouped under three categories (of perhaps decreasing difficulty): the first group encompasses a divine anger which Rudolph Otto described graphically in *The Idea of the Holy*: 'Something supra-rational throbs and gleams, palpable and visible . . . prompting to a sense of 'terror' that no 'natural' anger can arouse.'[4] We shall consider this anger in relation to the theory that the Jahweh of the Jews incorporated elements of a more primitive deity, a demon of the desert. The second group seems to portray God as a provoker of anger, an *agent provocateur* of violence, or (especially in the cases of Job and David) a tempter who provokes the faithful to rebellion. The third group, found most typically in the prophetic and apocalyptic literature, glorifies the warrior God, the destroyer of the ungodly, the avenger of the righteous.

Demon

The sheer horror of a divine wrath which cannot be explained – and probably cannot be contained – takes us back to the imagery of Hopkins' poem: 'lionlimb', 'darksome devouring eyes', 'turns of tempest'. Is this the despair which also lies behind Psalm 88?

> Thou has plunged me into the lowest abyss,
> in dark places, in the depths.
> Thy wrath arises against me.
> thou hast turned on me the full force of thy anger.
> Thou hast taken all my friends far from me,
> and made me loathsome to them.
> I am in prison and cannot escape;
> my eyes are failing and dim with anguish.
>
> Ps. 88.6–8 (NEB)

As we saw earlier (chapter one above) some incidents in the earlier parts of the Old Testament seem to portray a hostile god, whose anger or destructiveness has no clear justification. The attack on Moses at the night encampment (Exod. 4.24), the striking dead of Uzzah (2 Sam. 6.7) and the ordering of a census in order to give grounds for punishment (2 Sam. 24.1) are the most quoted examples. In addition, there are warnings of the uncontrollable character and excessive destructiveness of God's anger. For example, in Exodus 19.21f. the Lord warns Moses that the people must keep clear and the priests must consecrate themselves 'lest [the Lord] break out against them', and later the Lord promises to send an angel ahead to prepare the way to the promised land, but he will not journey with the Israelites, 'for fear that I annihilate you on the way; for you are a stubborn people' (Exod. 33.3 NEB). Such descriptions of the anger of Jahweh have led to the thesis of P. Volz (*Das Dämonische in Jahwe*)[5] that the achievement of monotheism in Israelite religion was brought about partly by incorporating in the one God more primitive elements, notably the unpredictable and frightening demons of the desert night and the gods of wind, storm, earthquake and fire (see Isa. 66.15; Jer. 23.19; Num. 16.1 – 35; Num. 11.1–3). Thus, according to Volz, we must see 'the demonic *in* Jahweh', a mysterious and frightening aspect which is not cancelled out by subsequent moralizing about his anger.

Such a view, however, would be contested by other Old Testament scholars. According to W. Eichrodt much can be explained as 'the vivid style of popular expression'.[6] He explicitly denies any suggestion of the demonic, claiming that, 'there can never be any question of despotic caprice striking out in blind rage'.[7] A more cautious judgement is offered by Lindström in his recently published exegetical study, *God and the Origin of Evil.*[8] Lindström analyses in detail the key passages or proof texts which are used to establish the demonic theory and concludes that other explanations are more plausible if the context is properly understood. In most instances a proper understanding of the cultic or propitiatory nature of the incidents shows them to be different from the warding off of evil spirits, associated with magical rites. Thus Lindström can assert that there is no evidence to suggest that Jahweh was seen as incorporating evil or being the cause of all evil, as an overemphasis on the monistic character of Jewish religion might suggest. Rather, the question remains unresolved between a monistic or a dualistic account: 'the Biblical texts provide no grounds for generalizing either one way or the other about the origin of evil'.[9]

Perhaps, then, it would seem that to call God's anger 'demonic' is an overstatement, or at least, that the evidence for evil intent and unpredictability is not conclusive. Nevertheless, this does not take away from the degree of fearsome violence in the God of the Old Testament (and to some extent of the New Testament also).[10] Even if all instances of this dangerousness can be accounted for either by the concept of the violation of the holy (cultic failure) or by moral transgressions, we are still left with the problem of 'overkill'. For those who incur Jahweh's displeasure the results are truly terrible: plague (Num. 11.33), drought (Deut. 11.17), famine leading to cannibalism (Lev. 26.29), burning and burial alive (Num. 16.31–5), and death by the tens of thousands (Num. 25.9; 1 Sam. 6.19; 2 Sam. 24.15). This destructive element is muted in the New Testament but is still evident in the apocalyptic material (Mark. 13.14–19 and par.; Rev. 14.9–11). We are reminded how frightening excessive anger in ourselves and in others can be. When such anger is linked with total power (as traditional accounts of the deity imply) it becomes truly fearsome. For here is that sense of chaos, that sense of a world irremediably out of control and under terrible threat, the dark vision of Yeats' 'Second Coming'. To see God as ruler of all is indeed to see him 'ride the wings of the storm' – but to what terrible purpose?

Tempter

This difficulty scarcely diminishes when we consider the God who is the *agent provocateur* of anger and violence in others. The story of Saul and Agag in 1 Samuel 15 provides an illustration. The Lord orders Saul, through his spokesman Samuel, to destroy the Amalekites utterly: 'Spare no one; put them all to death, men and women, children and babes in arms, herds and flocks, camels and asses' (1 Sam. 15.3 NEB). But Saul disobeys to the extent that he spares Agag, the king of the Amalekites, and also what his men regarded as 'useful', i.e. the best of the flocks. By this disobedience Saul loses his right to be king of Israel, and Samuel, the obedient servant of the Lord, makes good Saul's omission:

> Then Samuel said, 'Bring Agag king of the Amalekites.' So Agag came to him with faltering step and said, 'Surely the bitterness of death has passed.' Samuel said, 'Your sword has made women childless, and your mother of all women shall be childless too.' Then Samuel hewed Agag in pieces before the Lord at Gilgal.
>
> 1 Sam. 15.32–33 (NEB)

Such inclemency is surely familiar enough in tribal wars, but
what makes the passage notable is that in order to obey God
one must be willing to be so unremitting in violence. Saul's
clemency is seen as a flaw. Equally, God is to provoke the anger
of his chosen successor to Saul, David. We have already
referred to two strange incidents involving David, the striking
dead of Uzzah for accidentally touching the ark and the
ordering of a census which was to bring only punishment. In
the former incident David is made so angry and afraid (2 Sam.
6.8–9) that he leaves the ark aside until he can be sure that the
Lord is showing a more favourable face once more. In the
incident of the census David is trapped by the necessity to
obey. All that is then left to him is a choice of punishments:
three years famine, three months of flight from enemies or
three days of epidemic. David decides to trust the Lord's mercy
and chooses the epidemic. Whereupon seventy thousand of his
people die (2 Sam. 24.11–15). (It is interesting to note that the
Chronicler, perceiving the injustice in this story, alters it in one
essential detail. In a later version of the same story it is Satan
who wants to bring trouble on Israel (1 Chron. 21.1), not God.)

But if the Chronicler can 'improve' the theology of an earlier
period in the case of David, what could possibly be done with
the book of Job? For here God, at the very least, *permits* Job to
be tempted by the adversary or Satan. And if the prologue
(perhaps a later addition) appears to 'let God off the hook',
Job, provoked beyond measure, certainly does not. To him (as
we saw in the previous chapter), God is a 'soldier gone mad
with hate' who in anger tears him limb from limb. And Job
expects no justice from God:

> I am innocent, but I no longer care.
> I am sick of living. Nothing matters;
> innocent or guilty, God will destroy us.

> Job 9.21–2 (TEV)

Don't condemn me, God.
   Tell me! What is the charge against me?
Is it right for you to be so cruel?
   To despise what you yourself have made?
   And then to smile on the schemes of wicked men?
Do you see things as we do?

You know that I am not guilty,
 that no one can save me from you.

Job. 10.2–4, 7 (TEV)

Can't you see it is God who has done this?
 He has set a trap to catch me.
I protest against his violence,
 but no one is listening;
no one hears the cry for justice.

Job 19.6 (TEV)

Thus the ambiguity of the wrath of God remains. Does he tempt us, provoke us, incite us to violence, out of the violence of his own nature? Or is this a blasphemous calumny on the character of God? A. P. Hayman has explored this question in relation to the treatment of the problem of evil in Rabbinic Judaism and he concludes that there is an unresolved tension in the theology, related perhaps to the believers' uncertainty about the duality of their own natures, an uncertainty which they project on to God. God is portrayed as having two opposing attributes, justice and mercy, and the former is seen as 'an inexorable principle of retribution operating in the world, whose operations God must somehow prevent'.[11] God holds back his destructive anger against humankind but with difficulty. Thus the answer given in *b. Ber.* (7a) to the question, 'What does God pray?' is 'May it be My will that My mercy may suppress My anger . . . so that I may deal with my children in the attributes of mercy and, on their behalf, stop short of the limit of strict justice.'[12] It is a short step in this view of God, as Hayman observes, to the identification of the adversary (the Satan, the tempter) with that attribute of God which seeks punishment without mercy, God's justice. We are then back at the monistic account of evil referred to in the previous section. The development of this in the Kabbala clearly makes temptation to evil part of God: 'There is in God a principle that is called "Evil", and it lies in the north of God . . . for the *tohu* is in the north, and *tohu* means precisely the evil that confuses men until they sin, and it is the source of all men's evil impulses.'[13]

Avenger

So the question of theodicy will not go away, when we read of
the teasing anger of God. As Tevye, the Milkman, says as he
reflects on the futility of his dreams: 'But how is it said? *Life
and death issue from thine own lips.* When God sees fit to
punish a man he first takes away his good sense.'[14]

The dominant emphasis in the Old Testament, however, is
that evil is a human responsibility which amply justifies divine
wrath. God wreaks vengeance, not out of malice or evil intent,
but because it is against his nature to tolerate wrongdoing.
This is the emphasis in Jewish theology which Christian
theologians tend to favour, since it preserves God's moral
character. The responsibility for the anger lies squarely with
human beings who wilfully turn aside from the ways of God;
and God's chosen people, privileged as they were with God's
revelation and God's favour, merited the greatest retribution:

> For you alone have I cared
> among all the nations of the world;
> therefore will I punish you
> for all your iniquities.

Amos 3.2 (NEB)

Disobedience, especially that entailed in worshipping other
gods, gains immediate and wholesale punishment from the
jealous God of Israel (Exod. 32; Num. 16; Deut. 13.6–18; Josh, 7;
et passim). The prophets before the exile and the post-exilic
prophets see historical events as the clear evidence of God's
anger at his obdurate and unrepentant people:

> But your fathers would not listen; they paid no heed. They
> did not give up their wickedness or cease to burn sacrifices
> to other gods; so my anger and wrath raged like a fire through the
> cities of Judah and the streets of Jerusalem, and they became
> the desolate ruin that they are today.

Jer. 44.5–6 (NEB)

> Do not be angry beyond measure, O Lord,
> and do not remember iniquity for ever;
> look on us all, look on thy people.
> Thy holy cities are a wilderness,

Zion a wilderness, Jerusalem desolate . . .
After this, O Lord, wilt thou hold back,
wilt thou keep silence and punish us beyond measure?

Isa. 64.9–10, 12 (NEB)

But equally terrifying pictures of vengeful wrath are to be
found when the threat is not against Israel, but against her
enemies, the nations who oppose God's purposes. Here, in
magnificent poetic imagery, we have a fearsome avenger
indeed:

> With threats thou dost bestride the earth
> and trample down the nations in anger.
> Thou goest forth to save thy people,
> thou comest to save thy anointed . . .
> When thou dost tread the sea with thy horses
> the mighty waters boil
> I hear, and my belly quakes;
> my lips quiver at the sound;
> trembling comes over my bones,
> and my feet totter in their tracks;
> I sigh for the day of distress
> to dawn over my assailants

Hab. 3.12–13, 15–16 (NEB)

Such power to destroy is unleashed that, although it is
directed elsewhere, the prophet feels the awesome effect of it.

> The Lord is a jealous god, a god of vengeance;
> the Lord takes vengeance and is quick to anger.
> In whirlwind and storm he goes on his way,
> and the clouds are the dust beneath his feet.
> The Lord takes vengeance on his adversaries,
> against his enemies he directs his wrath;
> with skin scorched black, they are consumed
> like stubble that is parched and dry.

Nahum. 1.2, 11 (NEB)

Thus, although a justification is given for the fire, storm,
trampling and slaughter of the avenging God, it is hardly an
easing of the problem for those who see God as primarily
merciful. There is a boundlessness in the destructiveness which
is unleashed. This is the God who gathers all nations together to

let them feel the force of his anger, until 'the whole earth [is] destroyed by the fire of [his] fury' (Zeph. 3.8 TEV). In this third dark image of God's anger we find also connections with the New Testament, particularly with Romans and Revelation. In Romans 9 Paul confronts the problem of God's anger and God's mercy, especially as it affects the rejection of the people of the old covenant for the elect of the new. The answer he offers has led to much theological controversy: as a potter makes some treasured vessels and some for ordinary use, so God may reject the 'vessels of wrath', justly due for destruction, to 'show his anger and to make his power known' (Rom. 9.22 TEV). Equally, he reveals his glory in the mercy shown to those 'which from the first had been prepared for this splendour' (9.23 NEB) Here, clearly, we have the ambiguity revealed in the previous section of a God whose mercy cannot or will not hold back his wrath and whose decision to destroy some of his creatures is ultimately his responsibility as their creator. Thus the dark side of anger lurks still behind the God of the new covenant.

In Revelation, the perpetuation of the destructiveness of God's anger is evident in the writer's liberal use of Old Testament imagery. We encounter once more the cup of wrath, the consuming fires of wrath and the bloody picture of the grapes of wrath, first portrayed in Isaiah 63. The nations who oppose the lamb of God and worship the beast are utterly destroyed and the faithful rule in everlasting light in the new Jerusalem. As with the 'vessels of wrath' in Romans, so in Revelation the imagery of the 'wrath of the Lamb' causes problems to commentators. In particular Revelation 6.16 seems to portray a merciless and avenging Christ, as the mighty of the earth cry out to the mountains and the rocks, 'Fall on us, and hide us from the face of him that sitteth on the throne, and from the wrath of the Lamb' (AV). But some commentators on Revelation argue for a different view of divine anger, one which emphasizes the notion of self-inflicted punishment by those who cannot bear to see the merciful face of God. Thus G. B. Caird comments on this text:

They are men to whom a lie has become second nature, so that, faced with the love and forgiveness of the sacrificial Lamb, they can see only a figure of inexorable vengeance . . . To [them] no doubt the terror is real enough, perhaps even the only and ultimate reality; but it is nevertheless a travesty of the truth about Christ.[15]

In *The Wrath of the Lamb* A. T. Hanson has also argued for the essentially Christian use of Old Testament imagery in Revelation. According to Hanson the key to it all is to be found not in the blood of vengeance, but in the blood of sacrifice, the blood of the lamb that was slain. He sees all the portrayals of disaster in the Apocalypse to be a description of 'the working out in history of the consequences of the rejection and crucifixion of the Messiah',[16] and so the final message of the book to be one of the triumph of sacrificial love over all evil.

Such views may not fully answer the real difficulties facing us in this material but they do bring us to the other side of our exploration, the idea that the anger of God is, in Eliot's phrase, 'the unfamiliar Name' for love. Perhaps the dark shadow of destructive aggression emanating from divine wrath is just our limited view of the brilliance of divine love. In pursuit of this idea we may now lighten the picture by considering those biblical passages which stress the loving purpose of a God who seeks, not our destruction, but our wellbeing.

THE UNFAMILIAR NAME

In this section I shall describe three interrelated themes: the anger of the frustrated lover, the anger of the servant who seeks only to obey a loving master and the anger of the saviour in confronting the destructiveness of evil. Although I shall treat these separately, they are clearly interrelated, especially when we consider their relevance to an understanding of Jesus' life and ministry as a revelation of the nature of God.

Lover

The Jewish scholar, Abraham Heschel, in his account of the prophets of the Old Testament, has emphasized the total involvement of their God in human affairs: 'Never in history has man been taken as seriously as in prophetic thinking. Man is not only an image of God; he is a perpetual concern of God.'[17] It follows that, although God's anger can be harsh and dreadful, it is because his love is 'profound and intimate'.[18] He is angry in order to cancel the cause of anger and the ultimate secret of his anger is compassion. Thus anger is not a fundamental attribute of God, but 'a transient and reactive condition',[19] seeking the restoration of the beloved. So Hosea speaks of Israel as an unfaithful wife and of God as the patient lover whose loyalty knows no human bounds:

> How can I give you up, Israel?
> How can I abandon you? . . .
> My heart will not let me do it!
>   My love for you is too strong.
> I will not punish you in my anger;
>   I will not destroy Israel again.
> For I am God and not man.
>   I, the Holy One, am with you.
> I will not come to you in anger.

> Hos. 11.8–9 (TEV)

Here is the insight of Psalm 30.5 that, while God's anger may last for a moment, his goodness lasts for a lifetime (cf. Mic. 7.18). It finds an explanation for his anger as a 'wounded love', the zeal of the covenant God for the welfare of his people. Hidden in the terror of God's anger there is a love greater than any human love, if only we will cease our flight from his goodness and find our true peace (see Ps. 85). This is the paradox so evocatively described in Francis Thompson's poem, *The Hound of Heaven*:

> I fled Him, down the nights and down the days;
> I fled Him, down the arches of the years;
> I fled Him, down the labyrinthine ways
> Of my own mind; and in the mist of tears
> I hid from Him, and under running laughter.

But when the relentless pursuer finally succeeds he proves not frightening at all:

> Halts by me that footfall:
> Is my gloom, after all,
> Shade of His hand, outstretched caressingly?
> 'Ah, fondest, blindest, weakest,
> I am He Whom thou seekest!
> Thou dravest love from thee, who dravest Me.'[20]

And this realization that the supposed adversary is after all a lover who seeks only to evoke a response of love is also found in the last lines of Hopkins' 'Carrion Comfort' where, like Jacob at Peniel, he find he has been wrestling with his God:

> That night, that year
> Of now done darkness I wretch lay wrestling with (my God!)
> My God.

Yet we must avoid oversimplification of this insight into God's nature. The dangerous love of God which we find portrayed in the Old Testament cannot be reduced to the individual's religious experience, however poignantly described by Hopkins and Thompson. Rather it is the loving anger of a covenant God, seeking out a whole people, demanding a response from a whole people and punishing a whole people for the sins of some or all. It is God's chosen ones, God's favourites, who receive the full warmth of his love and, thereby, the full heat of his anger. This partiality of God, the zealous and jealous lover, cannot be evaded. The covenant God has a merely instrumental view of humankind outside the body of the elect. Gentiles may, like Cyrus, be used as the rod of his anger to punish disobedient Israel, but they remain strangers to his love. More must be added before the angry lover of the prophetic literature becomes the seeker after the wellbeing of all humankind. This move to impartiality in love and away from partiality towards a chosen people, entails a quite new image of God – that of a lowly, misunderstood and suffering servant.

Servant

To speak of the anger of God as the anger of a suffering servant takes us to the central 'offence' of Christianity – the *pathos* of God, the God whose love entails vulnerability, danger for the lover as well as the beloved. The power of God changes in character radically. In *Love's Endeavour, Love's Expense*, W. H. Vanstone describes well this 'precarious endeavour', of a God who empties himself for the sake of his creation:

> If God is love, and if the universe is His creation, then for the being of the universe God is totally expended in precarious

endeavour, of which the issue, as triumph or as tragedy, has passed from His hands. For that issue, as triumphant or as tragic, God waits upon the response of His creation. He waits as the artist or as the lover waits, having given all.[21]

Against this background of a God who takes risks we may begin to understand the rare instances of reported anger in the ministry of Jesus. Having rejected Satan's temptations to assume supernatural powers, Jesus accepts the powerlessness of the servant. He cannot compel obedience, loyalty, or even an understanding of what he is doing. But, inevitably, his servanthood provokes conflict. In obedience to the call of humanity rather than to the requirements of a self-righteous piety, he heals on the sabbath day. The failure of the people to understand the true meaning of the sabbath both angers and saddens him (Mark. 3.1-6, but note that Matthew omits all reference to anger and Luke transfers it to the Pharisees). Similarly, Jesus shows anger towards his disciples when they fail to understand that little children are closer to the Kingdom of Heaven than those adults who might suppose themselves close to it. (Mark. 10.13-16 – once again Matthew and Luke omit the reference to Jesus' anger).

Perhaps we can see in these disparities between the different synoptic accounts the uncertainties entailed in making God a servant. Holding on to the humanity of Jesus is not easy, when that same vulnerable person is seen as the Son of God, indeed as the revelation of the true nature of God. That perpetual riddle of Christian theology – how can true humanity and true divinity be combined in one individual? – tends to create a split in our understanding of Jesus, which is usually healed by a compromise regarding his humanity. Thus the passion narratives, influenced by the servant song of Isaiah 53, tend to emphasize the vicarious character of the death of Jesus – 'he was wounded for our transgressions . . . the Lord hath laid on him the iniquity of us all' (Is. 53.4-6 AV). Here is Jesus the passive victim, the lamb to the slaughter, taking the wrath of God on his own head, silent before his accusers as the sheep before the shearer is dumb, the quiet recipient of violence, who shows only forgiveness to his persecutors.

Yet around the edges of this picture of saintly resignation, there are glimpsed scenes of a quite different quality. What are we to make of Jesus' violent cleansing of the temple?; of his remark to the Pharisees about Herod, 'Go tell that fox . . .' (Luke 13.32 NIV)?; of his provocative denunciation of the Pharisees as 'whited sepulcres' and 'serpents' (Matt 23.27, 33 AV)?; of his conflict with his own disciples and his impatience with their misunderstanding of him (Matt. 16.23)? The totally passive Jesus may be a convenient device for a consistent 'penal substitution' theory of the atonement, but it fails to fit the impression of the real man which the gospels portray. Totally self-sacrificial anger, the anger solely for others without the assertion of and defence of self, is only partially true of Jesus. In the language of Revelation the Lamb is also wrathful and that wrath must be more fully understood if that which saves us in the anger of God is to be understood.

Saviour

A more dynamic account of the saving power of God's anger can be derived from a surprising source – the saying from the sermon on the mount which appears to condemn anger as equivalent to murder (Matt 5.21–22). The force of this text can be properly understood if we realize that it is part of the dramatic overturning of the security of abiding by the letter of the law, which is the effect of the entire sermon. Seen in this context, we realize that Jesus was no passive victim, enacting a foreordained death to pay God's penalty for sin. On the contrary, the true threat which came from Jesus was that he challenged fearlessly and with great passion the easy assumptions of a religion which thought it could assess sin and apportion blame. For Jesus, it was what lay in a person's heart that counted, not the outward respectability of behaviour. So anger and murder were in the same category. (Thus the New English Bible translation of the verb form, *orgizesthai* in Matt. 5.22 as *'nurses* anger' seems accurately to capture the spirit of Jesus' teaching. He was concerned with attitude, not simply with isolated action or reaction.) This perspective on the morally active ministry of Jesus allows us to see him as truly within the prophetic tradition, forthrightly denouncing those authorities, civil or religious, who substitute idolatry for the true religion and thus, not surprisingly, bringing retribution upon himself. Like Jeremiah before him, Jesus felt within himself the fire of God's anger: 'Your anger against them burns in me too, Lord, and I can't hold it in any longer' (Jer. 6.11 TEV).

But there is a final mystery in the anger of Jesus, the saviour, which renders a coherent Christology still more difficult. If aspects of Jesus' words and actions are reminiscent of Jeremiah, there are incidents in his last hours which are still more reminiscent of Job, the man in conflict with God. Perhaps this testing of Jesus beyond what is fair and reasonable is what the letter to the Hebrews refers to as, 'tempted as we are, yet without sin' (Heb. 2.18; 4.15 RSV). Does Jesus see the relentless tempter in God when, in Gethsemane, he pleads to be rescued from this approaching agony? Does he glimpse the demonic, the alien uncaring face of God, when in his dying moments he quotes words of bitter anger and despair from Psalm 22?

> My God, my God, why have you abandoned me?
> I have cried out desperately for help,
>   but still it does not come.
>
> Ps. 22.1 (TEV)

Here is the depth of the mystery that defies a tidy theological solution. The road to Calvary, entered out of love and passion for the truth, leads to a darkness where all that is left is anger against God himself, a final and terrible defeat of faith, before the words of trust can be uttered: 'Into your hands I commend my spirit' and the words of acceptance, 'It is finished'. Is this God against God? We recall the terrible risks described by Vanstone in the precarious endeavour of love. Perhaps then it is true that God is powerless against a destructiveness evident throughout history, not only in his creation, but also in his own nature, because finally his only weapon is the love which *we* must find and must still hope in, despite appearances that all is lost. If this is so, then that final anger of Jesus against the threat both to his life and to all he believed in, could be our only way of liberation – not resignation, but a rage that what is so precious can be so easily destroyed. Then, and only then, can be found an acceptance which allows us still to love.

THE PERSISTENCE OF HOPE

The outcome of this survey of the range and diversity of accounts of divine wrath in the Bible has been to confirm the suspicion that there are no easy answers to the problem of the seeming contradictions in God's nature and of the evident vulnerability of a reliance on love. In the final chapter of this book I shall return to the theological issues, relating them more specifically to the task of pastoral care. We can see at this stage, however, that anger leads in two different directions: the first is towards enduring hostility, summarized in the equivalence of anger and murder in the sermon on the mount. I shall look in greater detail (in the chapter which follows) at the way in which anger leads into this 'prison of hostility'. But the second direction is towards a freedom from that which oppresses us, a freedom gained by using our anger to bring about change in ourselves or in others. In chapter five I will explore this more positive possibility, the 'flying free' from the prison of our hostility and despair. But the persistence of hope entailed in this positive use of anger is not easily gained. It means trusting a saviour who seemed to lose everything, even the God in whom he trusted. The poet, James K. Baxter, seems to sense the quality of this persistent hope – 'as blind men meet and touch each other's faces' – when he reflects, in part of his 'Jerusalem Sonnets', that hope lies paradoxically in the final loss of power to control one's fate:

Colin, you can tell my words are crippled now;
The bright coat of art He has taken away from me

And like the snail I crushed at the church door
My song is my stupidity;

. . . . .
Prayer of priest or nun I cannot use,
The songs of His house He has taken away from me;

As blind men meet and touch each other's faces
So He is kind to my infirmity;

As the cross is lifted and the day goes dark
Rule over myself He has taken away from me.[22]

FOUR

The Prison of Hostility

I was angry with my friend;
I told my wrath, my wrath did end
I was angry with my foe;
I told it not, my wrath did grow.

William Blake 'A Poison Tree'[1]

Envy and anger shorten a man's life,
and anxiety brings premature old age.

Ecclesiasticus 30.24 (NEB)

Putting away falsehood, let everyone speak
truth with his neighbour . . .
Be angry but do not sin; do not let the sun
go down on your anger.

Ephesians 4.25–26 (RSV)

So far I have been directing my efforts towards severing the
'lethal link' between anger and destructive aggression, a
connection we can discern in both human and divine anger. But
now a contrary danger must be identified: if anger is denied
direct expression, then love can be undermined in more subtle
ways. We may speak of the 'prison of hostility' in which we
sometimes find ourselves. Because we have sought always to be
loving and considerate, whatever the provocation we have
received, we can suffer from physical illnesses associated with
stress, or we can feel resentful and unappreciated, or we can be so
depressed that we are incapable of love of self or of others any
more. Cast into a prison we ourselves do not fully recognize,
we wonder why we feel so hopeless, why the Christian life of
love seems so pointless in a world where few people can be

trusted for long and where everyone seems to be out for himself or herself. Thinking of ourselves as 'nice' people, we are yet in a state of semi-permanent hostility towards a 'nasty' world. How is such a prison created? And how may we escape from it, to gain a realistic appraisal of the relationships between ourselves and others?

I have already discarded the simplistic 'ventilationist' view that 'letting off steam' every time we feel angry will solve all our problems in human relationships and personal integration. On the other hand, people frequently allow anger to have destructive effects because, through a failure to understand – or even to acknowledge – the force of their own anger, they allow it by default to work negatively on themselves and on others. This hidden, unacknowledged power of anger is perhaps the major source of destructiveness in day-to-day human relationships. Its effects are less obviously damaging than the overt anger which leads to physical assault, but it is still a potent source of unhappiness and of ill-health. In order to understand what is happening, we need to use the rounded theory of the emotional state of anger which was outlined earlier (chapter two above). Anger is a blend of physiological reaction, immediate feelings and cognitive interpretation. Anger can be changed into an enduring state of destructiveness of self and of personal relationships when these aspects become disconnected or distorted in various ways, and when the anger is either denied, or displaced, or nursed into a condition of continuing hostility. I shall consider in turn each of these inadequate responses to anger and then suggest a way out of this 'prison' through the use of our awareness of being angry to improve communication with those who hurt or threaten us.

ANGER DENIED

There is a conceptual difficulty in the claim that anger can work covertly to undermine our health or our relationships with others, which must be dealt with first. If anger is, as I have argued, an interpretation of a state of physiological arousal, how can it work covertly? This difficulty is related to the general problem of claims about unconscious motivation, made so frequently by the advocates of depth psychology.

How can anyone know of the existence of an emotional factor operating within an individual, if that person has no awareness of it? Physiological changes can be monitored by an outside observer, and cues to emotion may be gained from facial expression, verbal postures, tone of voice, etc. But surely to say 'he is angry, although he is not aware of it', is, at best, an unverifiable inference and, at worst, a contradiction in terms. For, if the person is not aware of it, is 'it' really that blend of physiological arousal and cognitive interpretation we call 'emotion'? It could be argued that the 'although you think x, you really feel y' line of argument (in the style of the conversation in the café described in chapter two), is a way of stimulating a particular state, by encouraging an interpretation towards which the individual had no prior leaning. Thus Freudian or other psychodynamic 'explanations' of motivation could be seen as self-fulfilling prophecies. The interpretation offered helps to create the condition it describes as already present.

An alternative way out of the conceptual problem would be to reject the 'unconscious motivation' argument in favour of a description of different levels of awareness. This was what William James was attempting in speaking of the 'margins' of consciousness.[2] We are dimly aware of some aspects of our conscious experience, but we may only partly acknowledge them or we may quickly direct attention away from them because they are seen to be either a distraction or a source of anxiety which we wish to avoid. Thus, in the case of the physiological arousal associated with feeling angry, we may suppose that some people have learned (perhaps through childhood experience, perhaps through more general cultural conditioning) habitually to disregard the bodily changes caused by the physiological arousal or habitually to interpret them as a different emotion, for example, as embarrassment or generalized anxiety. This account would reject phrases like 'covert anger' or 'unconscious anger' in favour of 'avoided anger' or 'anger denied', since all the person has experienced (and this quite dimly) are the antecedents to anger. It is important to distinguish this avoidance or denial of anger from the shift in emotion which can occur when we realize, with full awareness, that our angry emotion is inappropriate because we have misinterpreted the situation. (For example, we might feel anger at a seeming insult, but then feel pleasure when we realize that the other person is joking with us in a friendly way.) It must also be distinguished from the conscious choice not to act aggressively, even although we feel, and fully accept that we feel, angry. 'Anger denied' happens at a less fully conscious and deliberate level. It is a habitual avoidance of the angry reaction to threat or frustration which our first response to a situation has prepared us for. It is an aborted emotional reaction at the margins of consciousness and barely within our control.

Physical Illness

This alternative explanation seems a fruitful one from the point of view of the physical disorder often ascribed to unresolved and unacknowledged anger. A long list of physical complaints has been suggested by some authors as the consequence of 'bottling up' anger. For example, Madow lists migraine and headache, ulcers, asthma, skin disorders, genito-urinary problems, arthritis, high blood pressure, angina, coronary thrombosis, severe depression and suicide.[3] The problem, however (as Tavris points out), is that anger, whether denied or expressed, is rarely separable from other emotions: 'our emotions are not especially distinctive. They tend to come in bunches like grapes, and it is very rare to find a single emotion causing trouble on its own'.[4] Tavris argues that the common factor in illnesses which appear to have psycho-somatic origins is unresolved conflict associated with a range of emotions, of which anger would be one.[5] This view would be supported by Buss's review of studies of anger in relation to psychosomatic illness.[6] Only two conditions seemed to be consistently associated with conflict (normally a sense of guilt or anxiety) over feelings of anger – essential hypertension and neurodermatitis. In hypertensives Buss suggested there was 'an intense approach-avoidance conflict concerning anger'[7] which resulted in a hypersensitivity to the physiological stimuli of anger. This heightened awareness served to maintain the physiological reaction of increased levels of adrenalin, which in turn maintained the blood pressure at a dangerously high level, leading to thickening of the arterioles in response to this pressure, which in turn required that the high pressure be maintained. In the case of skin disorders, Buss suggested that the rise in skin temperature associated with anger plus conflict concerning bodily appearance would provoke a discomfort leading to scratching and then to a chronic state of hypersensitive skin.[8]

Whether Buss's detailed explanations are correct, the general approach he suggests fits well with the idea that physical damage is caused by dysfunctional reactions to the antecedents of anger. The person who is made anxious by the bodily sensations signalling a possible reaction of anger, is caught in a spiral of denial of ever-increasing proportions, because, since the anxiety triggers those very physiological changes that are feared, that which is feared becomes harder and harder to keep to the margins of consciousness. Thus the person is maintained in a state of constant bodily tension with no outcome in releasing action. As we recall from the description in chapter two,[9] this will mean not only raised blood pressure, but faster breathing, tensed muscles, cessation of digestion and increased flow of acid in the stomach. It is not hard to see why a habitual avoidance of these reactions of the sympathetic nervous system – which serves only to increase them – leads to physical illness. It is not, however, the emotion of anger as such that is causing the trouble, but rather the fear of that emotion, which prevents any rational assessment of the bodily sensations and pre-empts any choice of action in response to an acknowledged feeling of anger.

Psychological Disorders

It has often been postulated that denied anger is also a major factor in pyschological distress, whether of a relatively minor kind or in the more serious form of an identifiable neurosis. Here the connection is made between unacknowledged anger and depression. In particular, depressive reactions to crisis like divorce, bereavement, illness and impending death have been traced to a failure to express anger.

It is inevitably much harder to draw a clear picture of how the physiology of anger might be related to pathological emotional states. Why should the failure to acknowledge or express anger lead to depression? There is no difficulty if we are prepared to accept Freud's later instinct theory in which a destructive force was regarded as endemic to organic life (see chapter two above). In this theory it is simply a matter of direction. If the death-instinct cannot find an 'outlet' in anger and aggressive acts then it turns inward creating guilt, depression and the urge to self-destruction. But we have seen that cognitive interpretation is such a powerful factor in human anger that the notion of 'instinct' fails to apply. More useful insights may be derived from two other quite different sources: the study of emotional reactions in young children and the evidence for the influence of hormonal changes in depression.

Taking the latter source first, it is now well documented that severe states of depression can result from imbalances in body chemistry. This is evident not only in cyclothymic (or manic-depressive) psychosis, where mood swings can be controlled by drug therapy, but also in depression associated with the hormonal changes after childbirth and at the menopause. Thus it is possible that the less extreme instances of failure to respond to physiological reactions to threat and frustration also create a biochemical imbalance leading to a depressive reaction. This might also serve to explain the reaction often described as 'passive aggression' – a numb and self-blaming state which seems at the same time to convey a powerful sense of anger at others.

But an explanation solely in terms of biochemistry is unlikely to do justice to the variability of human response to the universal experiences of loss, vulnerability and death. Why are some individuals more prone to depressive reactions than others? No one has been able to offer correlations between this variability and variations in individual biochemistry. A more promising line of explanation seems to be in terms of learned patterns of behaviour which may go back to experiences in early childhood. According to Storr:

> People who are liable to severe depressive reactions find difficulty in personal relations because they are ultimately looking for something which they should have had in infancy from their mothers, and which it is impossible for them to obtain in an adult relationship. Their personalities are formed upon the basis of

repressing and defending themselves against the intensely hostile feelings which the scars of infantile deprivation have left.[10]

This assertion sounds somewhat speculative, but some support for it comes from the work of Bowlby and others, investigating in great detail the effects of 'maternal deprivation' on infants and on their subsequent development in adult life. Bowlby's studies of the effects on infants of repeated separation from the mother (or from other significant 'attachment figures') showed a common pattern of intensely anxious and possessive behaviour with 'bitter anger directed against the attachment figure'.[11] Thus anger and anxiety are closely related, and the child who believes that a final desertion has occurred will quickly lapse into a depressed and apathetic state.

A particularly poignant example of these connections between anxiety, depression and anger is to be found in *Dibs: In Search of Self*, Virginia Axline's account of therapy of a child, so withdrawn that he was classified as mentally defective, yet who turned out to have an IQ of 168. It is hard to convey the atmosphere of this book in short extracts, but two examples of Dibs' spontaneously-composed songs and poems may reveal something of the child's world:

> He took a deep breath. Then he started to sing. He seemed to be composing the music, too. His voice was clear, melodious, and sweet. The music presented a contrast to the words he composed. His hands were clasped together. His expression was serious. He looked like a little choir boy. The words, though were not choir-boy words.
>
> 'Oh, I hate – hate – hate,' he sang. 'I hate the walls and the doors that lock and the people who shove you in. I hate the tears and the angry words and I'll kill them all with my little hatchet and hammer their bones and spit on them.' He reached down in the sand, picked up a toy soldier, pounded it with the rubber hatchet, spit on it. 'I spit in your face. I spit in your eye. I gouge your head down deep in the sand,' he sang. His voice rang out, sweetly and clearly, 'And the birds do fly from the east to the west and it is a bird that I want to be. Then I'll fly away over the walls, out of the door, away, away, away from all my enemies.'[12]
>
> . . . . .
>
> He . . . picked up the red paint. He brought this over to me, held it up, cupped between his hands. This time he spoke the words emphatically.

'Oh red, angry paint.
Oh paint, that scowls.
Oh blood so red.
Oh hate. Oh mad. Oh fear.
Oh noisy fights and smeary red.
Oh hate. Oh blood. Oh tears.'

He lowered the jar of red paint in his hands. He stood there silently, looking at it. Then he sighed deeply, replacing it on the easel. He picked up the yellow paint. 'Oh mean coloured yellow,' he said. 'Oh angry, mean colour. Oh, bars on windows to keep out the tree. Oh door with the lock and the turned key, I hate you, yellow. Mean old colour. Colour of prisons. Colour of being lonely and afraid. Oh mean-coloured yellow.' He put it back on the easel.[13]

When we hear Dibs' songs of hate and fear, we realize how hard it can be for a child to comprehend the turbulent feelings of anger and anxiety which well up, if – justly or unjustly – it seems that parents have abandoned them or do not really love them. The threatened child does not have the breadth of comprehension which can allow an adult to cope with separation and loss. Anger and anxiety – so closely related in terms of arousal – feed one another. It is too dangerous to be angry at those powerful figures who so easily abandon you. The child learns to favour anxiety and to withdraw from danger by blaming self. He finds himself locked in a prison, longing to fly free. Once learned, this pattern will return in adult life if the loss or the threat is sufficiently catastrophic. It is not a case of 'hidden anger' in many cases of depression after bereavement or depression at the prospect of death. Instead, anger seems not even a possibility. In its place is a well-established pattern of guilt and withdrawal. It is a long way back to the feeling of certainty about oneself that allows the churning stomach, the sweating palms or the racing pulse to be named as anger and for the source of that anger to be acknowledged in the full light of consciousness.

ANGER DISPLACED

Such is the power of anger, however, that it is rare for it to be totally unexpressed in any person's life. Even the individual who

finds such a surge of emotion embarrassing or frightening is
likely to have moments when angry words and an overwhelming
desire to some kind of physically violent action break through
the apparent calm. Then it is often the case that the anger is
displaced, since to direct it toward the true source of threat or
frustration would be too frightening. This is a common
experience for people suffering the shock of bereavement or
the deep anxiety of impending death. In *Death Comes Home*
Simon Stephens describes the grief of parents who lost their
young son suddenly and totally unexpectedly. They experienced
all the symptoms of what is now termed the 'grief reaction', the
psychological process of mourning which allows one to come
to terms with loss. Here is how Margaret, Joe's mother,
experienced anger:

> Why did her Joe have to die when he had so much to live for? Had
> she done something wrong for which God was punishing her?
> Perhaps it was because many years ago she had . . . but why Joe and
> not her? But if she wasn't to blame, who was? It was the surgeon!
> That was it . . . He was responsible for the lad's death. She would
> have legal redress! She would accuse him of criminal negligence!
> She would sue him for every penny that he possessed and have his
> name erased from the register of the Royal College of Surgeons.
> That's what she'd do!
>   But hadn't the Coroner returned a verdict of 'Accidental
> Death'? There was no question of criminal proceedings! . . . O
> God, why did it have to happen? Why did you take my Joe? Why?[14]

It is of course quite appropriate for Joe's mother to feel anger
at God and at the surgeon. They are the most obvious sources
of her hurt, and it may seem to ease the pain to hold them
responsible. But it is likely that there is a deeper pain in her
grief, one which she finds it hard to acknowledge. In tragic
bereavements like this one of the deepest sources of hurt is the
dead person himself. Margaret, Joe's mother, probably feels
abandoned by her dead son, and her anger at God and at the
surgeon is probably fuelled by an anger at her son, which she
cannot acknowledge because it seems so unreasonable, so
unfair. Yet it is likely to be there, at the margins of
consciousness, but kept from full awareness because of its
painfulness. Could she give it direct expression, it would help
her become reconciled a little more to her loss, but so long as it

is denied, there will be an unsurmountable, because unnamed, bitterness in Margaret's grief. Often in such situations the grief can become chronic, perpetuating a state of depression and making it difficult for the person to return once more to normal life.

In C. S. Lewis' *A Grief Observed* we also see anger at God, a God who often seemed 'a Cosmic Sadist':

> What chokes every prayer and every hope is the memory of all the prayers H. and I offered and all the false hopes we had . . . hopes encouraged, even forced upon us, by false diagnoses . . . by one temporary recovery that might have ranked as a miracle. Step by step we were led up the garden path! Time after time, when he seemed most gracious he was really preparing for the next torture.[15]

But Lewis is also able to tell his dead wife how much her death has hurt him: 'Did you ever know, dear, how much you took away with you when you left? You have stripped me even of my past, even of the things we never shared.'[16] The difference between the anger of C. S. Lewis and that of Joe's mother is an important one. Lewis, like Jòb, does not hesitate to accuse God. But Margaret fears to do this and so she looks for a sin in her past which can earn her God's punishment. Lewis can tell H. about his feeling of abandonment, but Margaret turns her accusations to a safer topic, medical incompetence. As we shall see later, when anger leads to direct communication like that of Lewis's, it is more likely to find a creative solution.

Another potent source of displaced anger is the testing experience of knowing of one's own impending death. In Elizabeth Kübler-Ross' famous work, *On Death and Dying*, there is a case description of a young nun whose awareness of her terminal illness made her – in the medico-nursing jargon – 'a management problem':

> She made it a habit while hospitalized to go from room to room, visiting especially sick patients and eliciting their needs. She would then stand in front of the nurses' desk and demand attention for these patients, which the nurses regarded as interference . . . Since she was quite sick herself, they did not confront her with her unacceptable behaviour, but expressed their resentment by making shorter visits to her room . . .[17]

In this description we see how both patient and nursing staff avoided direct expression of the anger they felt. They allowed it to be displaced into hostile behaviour which was sufficiently indirect to allow them to deny that they were angry. In a long counselling interview the nun finds the freedom to express some of her anger directly:

> Patient: I had to become what everyone wanted me to be. Now I don't any more. Now they have to learn to accept me, too. I *am* kind of demanding to them . . . People are angry at me and yet they made themselves angry. I didn't necessarily make them angry.
> Doctor: You are angry at people, too.
> Patient: Yes, I am . . .[18]

It becomes very clear in the interview with this Catholic sister that her difficulty in expressing anger directly is connected with her sense of being a nun, which is supposed somehow to dissipate her many resentments, against her family, against her fellow nuns and now against the hospital. This is a common problem within church communities of all denominations: Augsburger describes it as the problem of 'chronic niceness':

> Chronic niceness in a pastor tends to elicit comparable niceness in others, with the result that negative feelings are not readily shared and resentments accumulate. When the pastor's controls are finally overloaded, temper outbursts occur, with mixed results. While they may release momentary tension, they . . . further strain the relationship.[19]

It seems that churches have not always had such problems. By accounts of some previous ages, the problem was less one of 'niceness' than of restraining violence! We could take as an example John Galt's fictional (but probably not inaccurate) *Annals of the Parish*, depicting life in a Scottish parish in the eighteenth century. Mr. Balwhidder, having been placed in the charge by a patron, finds his induction a lively affair!

> The people were really mad and vicious, and flung dirt upon us as we passed, and reviled us all, and held out the finger of scorn at me; but I endured it with a resigned spirit, compassionating their wilfulness and blindness. Poor old Mr. Kilfuddy of the Braehill got such a clash of glar on the side of his face, that his eye was almost extinguished.

When we got to the kirk door, it was found to be nailed up, so as by no possibility to be opened. The sergeant of the soldiers wanted to break it, but I was afraid that the heritors would grudge and complain of the expense of a new door, and I supplicated him to let it be as it was: we were, therefore, obligated to go in by a window, and the crowd followed us in the most unreverent manner, making the Lord's house like an inn on a fair day, with their grievous yellyhooing. During the time of the psalm and the sermon, they behaved themselves better, but when the induction came on, their clamour was dreadful; and Thomas Thorl, the weaver, a pious zealot in that time, he got up and protested, and said, 'Verily, verily, I say unto you, he that entereth not by the door into the sheepfold, but climbeth up some other way, the same is a thief and a robber.' And I thought I would have a hard and sore time of it with such an outstrapolous people.[20]

The Twentieth-century successors of Mr. Balwhidder, ministering to a less 'outstrapolous' people, find it hard to tolerate anger in either themselves or others. H. A. Eadie, after a study of the psychological problems of Church of Scotland clergy, concluded that anger is an even greater problem for the modern clergyman than unacceptable sexual fantasies:

> aggressive impulses stimulate even greater anxiety and guilt in the clergyman. Any anger, hostility, or even competitive self-assertion, in himself or others, must be rigorously controlled and, if possible, rejected. These impulses, which are apparently in conflict with 'Christian' values of self-denial and non-aggression, are rejected by striving to attain the ideal of being a loving person.[21]

Perhaps it is such barriers to feeling in Christianity which led Nietzsche to describe it as the 'religion of resentment'. For the attempt to 'be nice' can lead to all the pettiness, feuding and backbiting which has been known in Christian communities since Paul's epistles (see, e.g. 1 Cor. 1.10–13; Gal. 5.15) In *Thus Spake Zarathustra* Nietzsche shows an acute awareness of the insincerity of much that claims to be friendship:

> Our faith in others betrays wherein we would dearly like to have faith in ourselves. Our longing for a friend is our betrayer.
> And often with our love we only want to leap over envy. And often we attack and make an enemy in order to conceal that we are vulnerable to attack.[22]

This is precisely the problem of displaced anger, whether in the personal setting of bereavement and terminal illness, or in the communal setting where 'niceness' is the order of the day: the anger which is expressed leads in a false trail away from its true source in our own fear of our vulnerable humanity.

NURSED ANGER

A third aspect of the harm which mishandled anger can cause is found in what might be called 'chronic anger', or more graphically 'nursed anger'. In Burns' 'Tam O'Shanter' we have an amusing description of such a nursing, as the wrathful wife awaits the return of her man who, sitting 'boozin' at 'the nappy', is 'getting fou and unco happy':

> We think na on the lang Scots miles,
> The mosses, waters, slaps, and styles,
> That lie between us and our hame,
> Where sits our sulky sullen dame,
> Gathering her brows like gathering storm,
> Nursing her wrath to keep it warm.[23]

Unfortunately, nursed anger is rarely so amusing, for it crosses a boundary between the immediacy of anger and the colder consistency of hostility and hatred. In *Understanding Anger in the Church* Bagby distinguishes anger from grudge-bearing or hatred. Anger he defines as 'an emotion springing from a *present* event, unnurtured or not cultivated, and without planned destructive intentions'.[24] In contrast, hatred is consciously sustained or nurtured, has an ongoing destructive intent towards a person and resists attempts at resolution. Similarly in *The Psychology of Aggression* Buss points out that the emotional reaction of anger must be distinguished from an attitude of hostility, which is 'an enduring response that builds up slowly and changes slowly. There is no tension state in hostility comparable to the physiological arousal of anger'.[25]

From the perspective of damage to one's own personality and to relationships with others hostility or hatred is clearly much more serious than anger. What I have called the 'nursing' of anger is, in more precise terms, the learning of a habitual response which, because is does not spring from any specific or immediate encounter with another person, is not amenable to change, except in the long term. Hatred has been well described by Max Scheler as a consistent policy of disvaluing that toward which it is directed.[26] Thus from this habitual response there comes the prejudice, stereotyping and especially the 'malignant aggression' described by Erich Fromm.[27] It is not in fact easy, *pace* Tam O'Shanter's dame, to keep one's wrath 'warm'! What can happen is that we lower our threshold for arousal, becoming irritable and short-tempered, because we have learned a pattern of interpreting our perceptions of others that portrays them always as aggressors or potential aggressors. (In its extreme form this pattern forms the basis for paranoia.) Alternatively – and still more dangerously – we may remain cool and seemingly detached, no longer feeling the arousal of anger. This is the frame of mind of the murder 'in cold blood', or, at a less serious level, of the person who must create unhappiness in others in order to feel vindicated. The danger lies in the sense of distance from the destructiveness which the absence of arousal creates, thus somehow absolving us from a sense of reponsibility. The heat of our immediate anger, although uncomfortable, is safer because it alerts us to what we feel like doing to others. As Louis MacNeice tellingly suggests in his poem, 'Brother Fire', a vicarious delight in that which destroys is not far from any of us:

> O delicate walker, babbler, dialectician Fire,
> O enemy and image of ourselves,
> Did we not on those mornings after the All Clear,
> When you were looting shops in elemental joy
> And singing as you swarmed up city block and spire,
> Echo your thought in ours? 'Destroy! Destroy!'[28]

ANGER EXPRESSED

It becomes essential, then, that we find ways of dealing with the arousal caused by the threats and frustrations of daily life which avoids the destructiveness of anger, denied, displaced or nursed into hatred. The key lies in realizing that human anger may be used to serve human ends. In particular, the specifically human capacities for verbal and non-verbal communication can be enhanced if we learn to use our anger constructively.

This is the insight contained in Ephesians: 'Therefore, putting away falsehood, let every one speak the truth with his neighbour, for we are members of one another. Be angry but do not sin; do not let the sun go down on your anger' Eph. 4.25–26 (RSV)

Modern psychological study of anger is confirming the wisdom of this ancient advice. A psychiatrist, A. Rothenberg, has pointed out that 'human anger occurs most frequently under conditions of need, love and involvement'[29] – in other words, we are 'members of one another', and the closer the involvement the more likely that we will feel anger. This means that anger can be used constructively or destructively within the context of this closeness. The destructive use is well-known – violent words or actions are used to cause as much hurt as possible to the instigator of our anger. But Rothenberg offers a constructive alternative: 'For humans . . . anger is an alerting phenomenon for the individual or for others that provides a basis for communication.'[30] In practical terms this means that either the angry person can respond to the situation by trying to explain the cause of his or her anger, or those around the angry person, seeing the anger in facial expression, voice tone, etc., can respond in a way that seeks to understand why the anger has been caused. Thus anger is made to serve better communication, without the reality of the anger being denied. Beverly Harrison makes the same point about communication as follows: 'Anger directly expressed is a mode of taking the other seriously.'[31]

An important aspect of this approach to the expression of anger is that it resists the simple 'tension reduction' or 'catharsis' interpretation popularized by followers of both Freud and Lorenz. Rather than anger being 'ventilated' like a build-up of steam, we must note the importance of the cognitive aspect of human anger. In perceiving 'I am angry', I perceive a complicated interpersonal situation and it is this I must seek to change if my anger is to be dissipated. Violent and uncontrolled aggression, verbal or physical, will not 'release' my anger. As we saw previously (chapter two above), it is just as likely to perpetuate it. Psychologist Robert R. Holt argues that the 'clearing of the air' that should occur has nothing to do with discharge of energy or reduction of drive tension. Rather: 'It refers to a cognitive clarification or restructuring that must take place before the instigation to anger is removed, without which anger will either remain or be transformed into hate.'[32] Of course, this does not imply a passionless discussion, since anger is essentially emotional in character and cannot be conveyed in a detached manner. But it does imply controlling the intensity of feeling in order to maintain contact with the other person, without denying the hurt and outrage one feels. It is this essential balance between reason and emotion which allows anger to be used in a uniquely human way, not to fight and not to flee, but to deepen love and friendship or to overcome injustice.

In the next chapter we shall consider how the liberation from the 'prison of hostility' which comes from the constructive use of anger can genuinely change things in both our personal lives and in situations of social and political oppression. Such liberation will not come easily, however. The prisons we make for ourselves, as well as those which others create for us, are not easily demolished. But perhaps it is a step in the right direction to see that love is better served when anger is neither feared nor denied, but given its place in our lives. In this we must disagree with the Christian poet, George Herbert:

> Be calm in arguing; for fierceness makes
> Error a fault, and truth discourtesy.
> Why should I feel another man's mistakes
> More than his sickness or poverty?
> In love I should: but anger is not love,
> Nor wisdom neither: therefore gently move.[33]

and see rather, a deeper wisdom in that tireless polemicist against Christianity, Friedrich Nietzsche:

> You should honour even the enemy in your friend . . .
> In your friend you should possess your best enemy.
> Your heart should feel closest to him when you oppose him.[34]

FIVE

Anger and Liberation

Do not go gentle into that good night
Rage, rage against the dying of the light.

Dylan Thomas[1]

Anger it was that won him hence
As only anger taught him sense.
Often my tears fall in a shower
Because of Anger's freeing power.

Stevie Smith[2]

We know through painful experience that freedom is
never voluntarily given by the oppressor; it must be
demanded by the oppressed.

Martin Luther King, 'Letter from Birmingham Jail'[3]

Stevie Smith's poem 'Anger's Freeing Power' describes a dream
of a pet raven, 'imprisoned' in a room with only three walls.
Despite her entreaties to the bird that it 'made a prison of a
place that is not one at all', and despite encouragement to fly
free through the open wall, it remains in its self-imposed
captivity. Only when two fellow ravens make it angry by
mocking its stupidity does the bird escape its prison:

And in my dream I watched him go
And I was glad, I loved him so,
Yet when I woke my eyes were wet
To think Love had not freed my pet.
Anger it was that won him hence
As only Anger taught him sense.[4]

After a long detour through biblical and psychological
accounts of anger, we must turn now to the practicalities of

dealing with our anger in such a way that it will set us free from the 'prisons' of hostility, depression and injustice which oppress us and our fellow humans. Stevie Smith's raven is caught in a prison of its own making: but there are those – like young Dibs, for example, who longs to fly away from his prison walls – who have been imprisoned by the failures of others to appreciate or understand their need. Thus I speak not only of 'freedom' from a prison, but of 'liberation', a word which implies a political act, changing oppressive conditions. We must not 'psychologize' anger to such an extent that it becomes merely a matter of the individual gaining insight and greater emotional maturity. Such gains are, of course, valuable, but they represent only part of the necessary response to anger, if it is to be creative. As we saw in the survey of biblical images of divine wrath (chapter three above), anger is closely related to prophecy, a demand for repentance and renewal. Thus we found in the anger of Jesus the prophetic fire of a Jeremiah, as well as the resigned wisdom of a Job who finally accepts God's will. The saviour who helps us live with the terror of the living God is also the servant whose anger for the oppressed and disregarded lashes out at the authorities of his day.

Thus this chapter is not merely about how to 'cope' with anger, as though there will always be a way in which, by adjusting our own emotional response, we can make human life tolerable. I shall discuss ways in which communication can be improved, when anger has been provoked, through acknowledging our anger, identifying its source, trying to understand the nature of the frustration or threat, and then finding ways of communicating with those who have made us angry that will avoid a cycle of mutual retaliation. But beyond these modifiable areas of human behaviour there lies more difficult territory: some situations are irremediable. Our own mortality or the mortality of those we love is perhaps the greatest source of threat and frustration in human life. Other situations are highly resistant to change. When injustice and exploitation are backed up by political might, what good can anger do? Here the question of liberation is a more complex one. It implies the persistence of hope, when things seem truly hopeless and only faith in the triumph of love over violence and destruction remains. This is a hard won liberation, and one which makes demands on us to care for all our fellow humans who are oppressed and in fear of death.

ACKNOWLEDGE, IDENTIFY, UNDERSTAND, COMMUNICATE

First let us consider how we may use anger more creatively in interpersonal relationships. The following situations represent some of the circumstances in which anger is commonly aroused in our day-to-day dealings with others:

Situation One
A person discovers that people have been talking about him to other people, saying things which seem unfair and which are calculated to cause derision or distrust. He reacts with a feeling of anger, related both to the unfair criticism and to the fact that it was 'behind the back'.

Situation Two
A teenager is criticized by a parent for breaking a family rule, e.g. coming home later than promised after a night out. The teenager retorts with angry defiance, which in turn provokes the parent's anger.

Situation Three
A person is passed over for promotion at work or in some way out-manoeuvred by a colleague. Anger is felt both because of the rejection and because of the impression that the less scrupulous one is, the more one seems to prosper.

Situation Four
Vandals break into a newly opened community centre in a housing estate. The local newspaper reports that furniture and pictures have been slashed, fixtures ripped from the walls, countless windows broken and various obscene slogans spray-painted on to the inside and outside walls. The seeming senselessness of it all provokes feelings of anger in the newspaper readers at the 'hooligans' responsible.

Situation Five
A casualty officer treats a baby brought into Accident and Emergency suffering from terrible injuries, apparently inflicted by one of its parents. The doctor feels anger against the person who could do such a thing to a helpless child.

Situation Six
A film, portraying poverty and malnutrition in a Third World country, is shown at a church meeting. It includes horrifying scenes of starving children and of homeless families struggling to survive. In the subsequent discussion a member of the audience comments: 'Why go on about these people? – they have only themselves to blame after all!' Several other people in the audience retort angrily to this comment.

We can notice at once two features which these six situations have in common: (1) A culprit or culprits can be identified against whom the anger is felt. Thus we are not dealing with denied or displaced anger of the kind discussed in the previous chapter; (2) None of the situations describes a simple threat or frustration of the type which might fit the 'fight/flight' reaction evident in animal behaviour. Rather, the anger is instigated because of the human capacity for interpretation and identification. In the first three situations threat or frustration is felt because of people's tendency to interpret non-physical events as dangerous, as threats not to life or physical safety, but to self-esteem. The gossip, the parental criticism and teenage defiance, the political manoeuvring are threatening because they undermine relationships upon which the threatened person depends. Thus, the interpretation of the events and of their significance in the individual's life is an all-important component in the arousal of the anger. So far as the second three situations are concerned, there is no direct threat to the people made angry, in either a physical or a psychological sense. Rather what is threatened are values which are important to them. (In this respect, Situation Four may be on a boundary between the two types of situation, since vandalism does contain an element of threat, but it probably provokes anger more because of the lack of community responsibility which it represents.) The last two situations in particular illustrate our capacity for identification with others which leads to anger on their behalf. We can feel arousal at injury or lack of concern which is not directed at us at all, and this again shows that human anger will not fit the simple pattern of flight or fight which may have been the origins of the anger-arousal system. The reflective ability of human beings and their wide-ranging imaginations create an immense range of possible instigations to anger. The more freely imagination ranges, the greater becomes the possibility for passionate arousal of all kinds. The difficulty of knowing how to deal with these emotional upsurges is part of the price we pay for being human rather than simply creatures of instinct and habit.

How is such anger to be dealt with in a liberating way? It might seem at a superficial level that the anger felt by the film audience, the casualty officer (and perhaps the newspaper readers) is 'better' than the anger in the first three situations, because it is on others' behalf and therefore more 'righteous', less selfish. But such a distinction is not a useful one when we are discussing the arousal of anger, although it can be more helpful in considering how one responds to that arousal. The moral justifiability of anger is really quite irrelevant to the simple fact that one's body is reacting in a particular way which is being felt as anger. As we have seen already, to deny this (out of anxiety, shame or fear of loss of love) is merely to store up trouble for ourselves, and probably also for others.

Acknowledge

The first step in a liberating approach to anger is to acknowledge our bodily response, without attempting to pass a moral judgement upon it. Paradoxically, this very acknowledgement can immediately cast the situation in a new light. For example, the recognition that we are becoming angry at a car which will not start, a door which is jammed or a train running late can help us see the humour in the situation and force us to look beyond the inanimate object to the true source of our frustration. Why are we so anxious? Why in such a hurry? Such reflection contributes a fresh interpretation to the bodily arousal, so that, rather than venting fury on the long-suffering car, house or railway system, we may come to recognize the undue pressure we are putting upon ourselves and try to find the source of our anxiety to be on time. In doing this we use interpretation to transform a potential angry outburst into an awareness of an anxiety which could be avoided. This transformation of anger can also apply to interpersonal situations where we feel ourselves threatened or devalued. The power of gossip, for example, is minimal on those who are willing to be honest with themselves about failures, but are also not afraid to recognize their own good points. Gossip is effective when it touches a person in areas of unadmitted weakness. It can be illuminating to ask oneself why it is that the criticism by others is sufficiently threatening to make us feel angry.

Identify and Understand

Thus, in addition to acknowledging the bodily arousal, it is important to identify its source and to try to understand why this particular event or relationship is so threatening or frustrating. As we have seen, these reflective moves can reveal that anxiety, not anger, is a better interpretation of our arousal and we can then attempt to deal with that. But this will not always be the case. It is not necessarily wrong or selfish of us to confirm our emotion of anger when we find ourselves threatened or frustrated. For example, the anger of the parent against the defiant teenager could be related (at least in part) to insecurity in the parent about his or her ability to be a parent; and the anger of the disappointed careerist (Situation Three) could reflect undue concern for self-esteem through social recognition. But it is as valid for these people, on reflection, to feel confirmed in their angry reaction. The trust and mutual respect upon which their family or work relationship depended has been broken. The angry reaction serves the purpose of telling the other person that this has happened and that the angry person is not prepared to accept such behaviour. (This kind of direct and emotional honest response can be very important for teenagers in particular, as they struggle to find a new relationship with their parents. A cool, over-reasonable or self-deprecating response from the parent can be more difficult for the young person to understand and cope with.)

Communicate

If then we have acknowledged an angry reaction, identified its source and recognized the threat of frustration which makes the anger appropriate, we are still left with the question of how anger is expressed. An academic discussion of this kind must make it appear that all this takes place in a leisurely fashion with ample time for reflection and planned responses. Real life, of course, is rarely like this. As all the vocabulary of anger indicates, people experience it as a boiling up (and over), a bursting out, a fiery flash, a choking or swelling leading to convulsive action. The most common experience of anger is that it is a loss of normal control which leads to words or actions which are subsequently regretted. As Horace put it: 'anger is a brief madness'.[5]

It can be argued, however, that these experiences of unbridled rage are the consequence of our anxiety about giving anger *any* expression, an anxiety which effectively fuels our bodily responses to a point where the final effects *are* overwhelming. (I am speaking here still of everyday experiences of anger. The kind of murderous rage which is sometimes associated with sadistic killing and other violent acts requires a stronger explanation than this.)[6] If we are unsure about how to express anger except in a way that causes damage to relationships, then we will be ill-prepared for rapid decisions about what to do when anger is provoked. In this context we must return to the observations of Rothenberg and Holt summarized in the previous chapter. A constructive use of anger entails using it in the service of better communication. Hoffman *et al.*, in a discussion of the growing practice of 'assertiveness training', have pointed out that a weakness in this approach is that it stresses the value of outspokenness without considering the effect of this outspokenness on those who are the recipients of it.[7] (The issue might be rephrased in biblical language by asking how we 'speak the truth in love' in a way which protects and promotes that love.) The difficulty lies, to a large extent, in the tendency for the expression of anger to constitute a threat to the other person, who may then respond with anger or with denial, either of which tends to obscure the real issue. Thus there ensues either an unproductive circle of mutual retaliation, or the retreat of the recipient of the anger from any direct communication. The alternative to this unproductive form of communication is for the person expressing the anger to avoid the temptation to attack in order to cause pain as a punishment for the pain he or she has experienced. Instead we can learn to express as clearly and forcibly as possible what it is we are feeling, what specific event has made us feel that way and what we expect from the other person in the relationship. Generalized accusations, character assassinations and emotional blackmail need to be avoided, if the expressed anger is to serve the purpose of love.

Let us imagine two different responses by angry parents to the defiant teenager, in Situation Two (see p. 68 above):

Response A
That's typical of you! You have no consideration of anyone around here and no respect either. You take everything and give nothing. I would never have spoken to my father [mother] like that, but you young people couldn't care less what you do. OK, be like that – but not in *my* house. I want an apology *this minute* or you can clear out. See if life is better outside than the cushy number you have here.

Response B
I feel angry (and a bit hurt too) when you shout back at me like that. Since we agreed together on a time for coming home, I think you should respect it or at least explain what kept you late. Let's not make a big thing of it tonight. Since I felt worried about you I'm probably over-reacting – and you look tired too. But I want us to talk this over again before your next night out.

Response A can lead only to either another outburst from the teenager or (more likely) a sullen silence and a refusal to confide in this parental 'enemy'. Response B does not deny the parent's anger, but it might help to defuse the immediate situation and it paves the way for more discussion when both parties feel calmer and less tired. Such a simple categorization of 'good' and 'bad' responses, however, could be misleadingly simple. There are many situations in which the possibility for a direct and creative discussion is remote. How does one deal with a manipulative colleague (Situation Three) without an atmosphere of accusation and without being accused of 'sour grapes'? In such situations, as probably with the malicious gossips, the relationship itself is too tenuous to allow for a creative use of anger. But the resources of a friend, or possibly a counsellor, can be called on to help the angry individuals express their anger articulately and clarify what they may realistically expect from the relationship and how they may achieve that. The least productive outcome is that of 'nursed anger', when all that emerges is a resentment constantly seeking instances of its justification (see chapter four above).

But a different problem arises when we consider the anger felt in situations four, five and six, anger at vandals, at child battery and at insensitivity to injustice. The difficulty here is that an expression of anger, however well articulated, is unlikely to change the situation for the better. The doctor's anger will not undo the battering of the child and is unlikely to prevent it in the future; the anger of the law-abiding citizens at 'hooligans' does nothing to reduce vandalism; and those who are convinced that the poor get what they deserve are unlikely to heed the angry reaction of people they regard as 'wishy-washy liberals'. The problem is one of appropriate and effective communication. Anger in the context of personal relationships can be more painful, but at the same time it is more potentially redemptive. The angry person has an enduring connection with the other person and can use this as a basis for direct communciation. But when people are strangers, or are alienated from one another by social or political forces, then the expression of anger can merely increase a sense of enmity and of distance between them. Yet to fail to express our outrage when values which we cherish are threatened is to be lost in an apathy which diminishes us. Beverly Harrison worries about the lack of anger in church life, suggesting that 'we Christians have come very close to killing love precisely because anger has been understood as a deadly sin'.[8] This is the 'chronic niceness' of which Augsburger speaks,[9] and its cloying effect diminishes both us and our fellow humans who suffer from our failure to protest in an articulate and politically effective manner on their behalf. In this context, some hard comments by a Maori woman about the lack of anger at racial injustice by the Pakehas (white New Zealanders) hits the mark precisely:

> The experience I've had is that Pakehas get off on Maori grief and anger. They feel guilty and angry when we spill our guts but they never feel inspired to *do* anything about it!
>
> Every Maori I know, every black I know, is a walking explosion. You just prick it and it's there. But a Pakeha . . . you've got to drag it out, kick them, beat them and they would only say, 'I feel so ashamed'.[10]

Thus we must find a way of moving from 'niceness' and guilt (which effectively prevent change) to a bolder confrontation of those forces which threaten to destroy all human value. For people with religious belief, the courage and articulateness may come if they are prepared first to face their uncertainties and fears about the love and justice of the God they worship, that area of darkness which we discovered when we surveyed the anger of God portrayed in the Bible (chapter three above). Dylan Thomas, pleading with his father to rage against 'the dying of the light', cries to him, 'Curse, bless me now with your fierce tears, I pray'.[11] When we consider the frailty of human life and the many ways in which love is lost in the tumult of war and the ravages of human greed, we too need that curse-blessing. To escape from our apathy, we shall need to learn to rage against our God.

THE DYING OF THE LIGHT

Consider, first, the anger of Ian Crichton Smith as he depicts the indignity of senility, in his poem 'Old Woman':

> And she, being old, fed from a mashed plate
> as an old mare might droop across a fence
> to the dull pastures of its ignorance.
> Her husband held her upright while he prayed
>
> to God who is all-forgiving to send down
> some angel somewhere who might land perhaps
> in his foreign wings among the gradual crops.
> She munched, half dead, blindly searching the spoon.
>
> Outside, the grass was raging. There I sat
> imprisoned in my pity and my shame
> that men and women having suffered time
> should sit in such a place, in such a state.[12]

The target of Crichton Smith's anger is the unreal God, pathetically prayed to by the woman's husband. So too, in the greater horror of the trench warfare of World War One, Siegfried Sassoon looks for an *effective* God:

> Deep in water I splashed my way
> Up the trench to our bogged front line.
> Rain had fallen the whole damned night.

> Oh Jesus, send me a wound to-day,
> And I'll believe in Your bread and wine,
> And get my bloody old sins washed white![13]

In Wilfred Owen's poetry, God is seen as an untrustworthy ally:

> I dreamed kind Jesus fouled the big-gun gears;
> And caused a permanent stoppage in all bolts;
> And buckled with a smile Mausers and Colts;
> And rusted every bayonet with His tears.
> And there were no more bombs, of ours or theirs
> Not even an old flint-lock, nor even a pikel.
> But God was vexed, and gave all power to Michael;
> And when I awoke he'd seen to our repairs.[14]

In grief, too, the sense of anger at God can be great. Here is how this is expressed by C. S. Lewis in *A Grief Observed*:

> Already, month by month and week by week you broke her body on the wheel whilst she still wore it. Is it not yet enough?
>   The terrible thing is that a perfectly good God is in this matter hardly less formidable than a Cosmic Sadist. The more we believe that God hurts only to heal, the less we even believe that there is any use in begging for tenderness.[15]

As we observed in the previous chapter, the most painful aspect of anger in bereavement is that which is felt against the dead person, and so sometimes anger against God is really a displacement of this too painful anger. But is it necessarily always and only that? Is it blasphemous and a denial of God that we express our anger when death threatens us or when it takes those we love? Wilfred Owen captures well the seeming mockery of prayer when death's terrible harvest is reaped in war:

> 'Oh! Jesus Christ! I'm hit,' he said; and died.
> Whether he vainly cursed or prayed indeed,
>   The Bullets chirped – In vain, vain, vain!
>   Machine-guns chuckled – Tut-tut! Tut-tut!
>   And the Big Gun guffawed.[16]

Perhaps there is more liberation in such anger at God than there could ever be from the pious consolations of a religion which does not see the depths of the tragedy in human life.

This is certainly a part at least of the message of the book of Job and it is also a prominent element in the laments in the Psalms, which come close to cursing God for his lack of care. If anger is the other side of love, then it must at times be a feature of a living faith, as opposed to a merely conventional religion which observes the niceties of good manners to the almighty.

In a poem entitled simply 'They', Sassoon bitterly exposes the humbug of the religious blessing on the war:

> The Bishop tells us: 'When the boys come back
> They will not be the same; for they'll have fought
> In a just cause; they lead the last attack
> On Anti-Christ; their comrade's blood has bought
> New right to breed an honourable race.
> They have challenged Death and dared him face to face.'
>
> 'We're none of us the same!' the boys reply.
> 'For George lost both his legs; and Billy's stone blind;
> Poor Jim's shot through the lungs and like to die;
> And Bert's gone syphilitic: you'll not find
> A chap who's served that hasn't found some change.'
> And the Bishop said: 'The ways of God are strange!'[17]

Similarly, in Kübler-Ross's book, *Living with Death and Dying*, we read of the anger of a nurse when a priest attempts some apparently trite consolation: 'One night after a long, unsuccessful fight to save a patient, a nurse overheard the family priest say to the relatives, "Well, it was God's will." The nurse blew up and stormed out of the department.'[18] Who is to say, in a situation of struggle for life or in a situation of coming to terms with a tragic and seemingly unnecessary death, at whom one's anger must be directed? It is a strange piety which forbids any anger against God for fear of causing offence. The frustration or the threat in such situations are real enough; the severe physiological reactions of fear and grief are totally to be expected and cannot be by-passed; the puzzlement and sense of betrayal in the person who put their trust in a loving God is easily understood, as Lewis so well illustrates. What then is the justification for insisting that people find an interpretation which will direct any anger they feel against God to some other target (probably to themselves)? Rather, such anger is best understood as the cry of someone who will not despair of God, who must struggle to continue to communicate with him, even through grief or fear. Such anger shows a trust still in God's goodness, despite the darkness of his face. Thus anger at the dying of the light shows yet more vividly how much we are children of light and not of darkness. Anger is the undefeated messenger of hope.

CRY RAGE

It is from such a perspective that we must return to the vexed topic of the use of anger to overcome injustice and to seek, behind the face of the oppressor, the face of fellow humanity. The seemingly intractable problem of racial discrimination provides vivid examples of the problem and of attempts to bring about change through non-violent protest. In the poetry of the 'coloured' South African, James Matthews, we experience a sense of hopeless rage at the unbridgeable gap between oppressed and oppressor:

> Can the white man speak for me?
> can he feel my pain when his laws
> tear wife and child from my side
> and I am forced to work a thousand miles away?
> . . . . .
> Can the white man speak for me?[19]

Matthews can feel at one only with his fellow blacks throughout the world:

> I share the pain of my black brother
> and a mother in a Harlem ghetto
> with that of a soul brother in Notting Hill
> as I am moved from the land I own
> because of the colour of my skin
>
> . . . . .
> Now our pain unites us
> into burning brands of rage
> that will melt our fetters
> and sear the flesh of the mockers
> of our blackness and our heritage.[20]

No one who knows the oppressive and unremitting injustice of the South African racial laws could blame Matthews for his anger and despair. In the context of racial discrimination in the USA, James Baldwin writes powerfully of the terrible history which has written, deep in the negro's soul, hatred for the white oppressor:

> This past, the Negro's past, of rope, fire, torture, castration, infanticide, rape; death and humiliation; fear by day and night, fear as deep as the marrow of the bone . . . rage, hatred, and murder, hatred for the white man so deep that it often turned against him and his own, and made all love, all trust, all joy impossible . . .[21]

Is there any way forward from such rage, a way which does not lead to hatred and to counter-violence? Baldwin sees quite clearly the difficulty: 'It demands great spiritual resiliance not to hate the hater whose foot is on your neck, and an even greater miracle of perception and charity not to teach your child to hate.'[22] And yet he can also write these words of hope to his imprisoned nephew appealing to a common humanity: 'But these men are your brothers – your lost brothers. And if the word *integration* means anything, this is what it means: that we, with love, shall face our brothers to see themselves as they are, to cease fleeing from reality and begin to change it.'[23]

Oppressed and Oppressors

In these words of Baldwin we begin to see why the anger of the oppressed must never be deplored or denied. Like the anger of the religious person against God, it is a sign of hope, of faith that one's fellow human beings can be made to listen. In his 'Letter from Birmingham Jail', Martin Luther King endeavoured to explain to a group of fellow clergymen why it was necessary for him, as a Christian minister, to disobey the authorities and force a confrontation leading to his arrest: 'Non-violent direct action seeks to create such a crisis and foster such a tension that a community which has constantly refused to negotiate is forced to confront the issue . . . there is a type of constructive, non-violent tension which is necessary for growth.'[24] King's experience as a Christian minister in confrontation with unjust authorities is being repeated in South Africa at the present time – by Desmond Tutu, Alan Boesak, Byers Naude and many other Christians, ordained and lay. It is vital to see that their anger against oppression is a genuine attempt to prevent revolutionary violence by trying to force the authorities to think again about their policies. Since personal communication has had no effect, they use political communciation, designed to provoke change yet seeking to avoid retribution and violence by the oppressed against the oppressor. Thus it is love's hard way, hard in the sense that it will make no concessions to injustice: but hard also for those who follow it, as the death of Martin Luther King illustrates. For the demand on those who follow in this way is that they abandon defence of self, even the vindication of the self in a moral sense. Communication through non-violent confrontation demands spiritual discipline, as both Gandhi and King constantly stressed. As soon as the protestor becomes self-righteous and lacking in awareness of his or her own fallability, then the appeal to a common humanity is lost. We all oppress others in our own way; and so we all need liberation from our hostility and aggression toward others. It is in this spirit of repentence, as Thomas Hanks stresses, that the Christian seeks justice:

> All of us are simultaneously oppressed and oppressors (Acts 10.38; Rom. 3.23) Satanic oppression occurs not only on the level of economic class struggle, but in all areas of human life . . . Thus the first step in genuine Christian discipleship is humbly to recognise my own situation: I am an oppressed oppressor.[25]

The Fire Next Time?

This quotation conveys well the tension in which we must live if we are to both retain our anger at oppression and find a way to speak to others as fellow brothers and sisters, whose oppressive tendencies we find in ourselves. As Matthews observes, the mere offer of 'dialogue' is no true answer to injustice:

> Dialogue
> The bribe offered by the oppressor
> glitters like fool's gold
> . . . . .
> the oppressor sits secure with his spoils

with no desire to share equality
leaving the oppressed seeking warmth
at the cold fire of
Dialogue.[26]

Instead, we must use the power of our anger to insist upon a true meeting, where, like the covenant God who will not relinquish his beloved, or like the suffering servant whose honesty brings out the truth in others, we want the other to change, for our sake and for theirs. This is the anger which seeks love, not destruction, and (as Baldwin conveys in a telling biblical image) it is the rainbow sign of liberation which all humanity needs, if we are to avoid 'the fire next time':

[we] must, like lovers, insist on, or create, the consciousness of others . . . If we do not now dare everything, the fulfilment of that prophecy, recreated from the Bible in song by a slave is upon us: *God gave Noah the rainbow sign, No more water, the fire next time!*[27]

SIX

The Fire of Love

If the eternal wrath were not, the eternal joy also would not be; in the light the wrath is changed to joy; the wrathful fire's essence is mortified as to the darkness in the wrathful fire, and out of the same dying the light and love-fire arise; as the light burns forth from the candle, and yet in the candle the fire and light are but one thing.

Jacob Boehme[1]

The love of God is not more real than the wrath of God. For He can be really angry only with those He loves.

P. T. Forsyth[2]

We only live, only suspire
Consumed by either fire or fire.

T. S. Eliot, 'Little Gidding'[3]

In our tortuous route through anger's strange country we have met many angry characters. Now, as the question of an adequate pastoral theology of anger arises once more, it is important to remember their many and varied responses:
- Ronnie Laing, the young medical student, watching with horror and rage the agonizing death of a child.
- Don Camillo, furious with his arch-enemy, Peppone the Mayor, but not getting much sympathy from Christ!
- Bernard Häring, in courageous and effective anger at the SS Colonel about to hang soldiers accused of cowardice.
- Tevye, the milkman, losing patience with God for making him poor, while other Jews are rich.
- Ian Crichton Smith angry at the sight of the senile old woman pathetically cared for by her husband with his false piety.

- The woman in the café, determined to find anger beneath her friend's grief.
- C. S. Lewis seeing God as a 'cosmic sadist' torturing him and his dying wife with false hopes.
- Dibs, with the choirboy's voice, singing of hate, killing and the longing to be free.
- The 'difficult' nun, angry in her dying days, refusing to be 'nice' any more.
- Thomas Thorl, the weaver, telling Mr. Balwhidder that he is a thief and a robber and not the true shepherd.
- Tam O'Shanter's wife 'nursing her wrath to keep it warm'.
- Titiwhai Harawira, the Maori woman, angry at the Pakehas for letting *her* be angry *for* them.
- Stevie Smith, weeping because anger, not love, set her raven free.
- James Matthews, crying with rage at white oppression.
- Siegfried Sassoon, asking Jesus to make himself useful and at least give him a wound.
- James Baldwin, hoping to overcome anger and hatred, but fearing the fire next time.

And alongside these expressions of human anger we must put the ambiguity of God's anger – the fearsome face of demon, tempter, avenger: the inspiring face of lover, servant, saviour. Can we, in the midst of all this complexity, find some kind of unity which will guide and sustain the pastoral task of understanding and using creatively the anger we encounter in ourselves and others? How are we to live with human anger and with the anger of God?

I shall seek an answer to this question by returning to the story of Job, the man angrily challenging God to explain himself. Job did not expect an answer, nor indeed did he receive one which in any way met his desire for an explanation. Job knew only too well the inequality of the contest in which he unwittingly found himself: 'He is not a man as I am, that I can answer him or that we can confront one another in court. If only there were one to arbitrate between us and impose his authority on us both' (Job 9.32–3 NEB). Yet there has been no shortage of 'answers' to Job from his fellow humans. I shall consider three of these: The first, which can be summarized as

'God in Man's image', argues that human pathology is the source of all negative aspects of anger; the second 'answer', which can be summarized as, 'Heads God Wins: Tails We Lose', seeks to hold on to the negative aspects in our picture of God, but justifies them all as reactions to human failure; the third 'answer', which can be summarized as 'Beyond Good and Evil', puts the anger of God beyond rational explanation, seeing moral categories as inadequate descriptions of the divine nature. Dissatisfied with all of these 'answers', I shall then conclude by offering as an alternative a living, dynamic view of God, which sees our struggles to live with his reality as getting in contact with 'the fire of love', a fire we also touch when we seek to live fully and honestly with our fellow human beings.

'ANSWERS' TO JOB

God in Man's Image?

In confronting the problem of human aggression (chapter two above) we have seen something of the depths of human violence and destructiveness. Thus it need come as no surprise that some people need a violently angry God, either as a justification for their own aggressive tendencies or as a target for the anger they dare not direct elsewhere. J. H. Kahn's extensive study, *Job's Illness: Loss, Grief and Integration*, offers an answer of this kind to Job's frantic questioning of God.[4] Kahn compares Job's state to a clinical depression which originates in his 'perfectionism' and he traces in a detailed (and remarkably persuasive) manner the psychological and physical symptoms in Job which support this comparison. In addition to skin disease, digestive problems and insomnia (30.30; 6.7; 7.3–4), Job – according to Kahn – manifests listlessness, obsessive behaviour and paranoia. Thus Job's anger at his comforters and at God is a symptom of the deep depression into which he has fallen as a result of the terrible losses he has sustained. The fearsome God who attacks him 'like a soldier gone mad with hate' (16.14 TEV) is a product of this disturbed state. The God who appears in a whirlwind comes to Job 'in the tempest of the mind'. We find a similar explanation to that of Kahn (but in a much briefer compass) in R. G. Collingwood's discussion of passion. Collingwood sees the book of Job as a transition from a religion of fear to a religion of anger. Moreover, he believes that in Christianity this transition finds its fullest expression: 'It is the essence of Christianity that . . . Christians should vent their wrath . . . upon God's own wounded head.'[5]

A theological account parallel to these explanations is given in Nicolas Berdyaev's discussion of the interaction between the Holy Spirit and the human spirit. According to Berdyaev, 'The light of absolute truth is refracted as it passes through the distorting medium of human nature'[6] and in addition God is compelled to conceal himself, since the full intensity of divine light would merely blind the beholder. A consequence of this is that Jahweh, the God of the old covenant, is not a revelation of the inner secrecy of God, which had to await the coming of the Son, and even that revelation was a penetration of the light 'only by degrees and . . . distorted by the medium which receives it'.[7] These observations allow Berdyaev to conclude that the wrath of God depicted in the Old Testament is simply a reflection of the wrath of the Jewish people. The God who reveals himself in the Son is infinite love: 'Anger in every shape and form is foreign to God, Whose mercy is infinite'.[8]

Berdyaev concludes that people need the concept of an angry God who must be appeased by a sacrifice, not because that is the nature of God, but because human beings, in their pride, are incapable of forgiving themselves. They need an angry God in order to keep punishing themselves. They are incapable of accepting a God who loves without conditions and who pardons absolutely. The psychoanalyst I. D. Suttie makes very similar observations to these in his famous work, *The Origins of Love and Hate*:

> Certain writers are evidently dominated by an intense sense of separation, with consequent guilt and anxiety, which preoccupies them with the problem of sin and redemption . . . and conceives God as terrible, man as vile . . . The supreme miracle of forgiveness is only credible to such minds as an adjunct to vicarious vengeance, and even so can only be enjoyed under precarious conditions or as an act of pre-destination of an entirely autocratic nature.[9]

There is undoubtedly an attraction in finding a way out of

the puzzle of the angry God by this route. The sheer vindictiveness in much of the Old Testament's descriptions of God's wrath (and in some of the New) can scarcely be gainsayed. Are we really called upon to emulate, obey or worship a God who exults in the slaughter of his enemies and who punishes the malefactor without mercy? Such a God seems indeed in a different religious universe from the God whom Jesus obeyed by showing love and forgiveness to his accusers, torturers and executioners. On the other hand the escape route via a theory of projected aggression seems a little too easy. If we take this escape route for the unacceptable angry God, how do we avoid Freud's analysis of our loving God as a projected ideal father, the product of our insecurity, believed in because he fulfils our most insistent wishes? Moreover, can we honestly say to Job that his anger is just a symptom of his reactive depression, which he will get over in time? This seems as bad, if not worse, 'comfort' than that offered by the biblical comforters! Job believes himself to be grappling with a real assailant, not a product of his distressed state – that is of the *essence* of his faith!

Such answers to Job, then, seem too facile, somehow diminishing both God and the believers. But, viewed against a full account of the relationship between anger and aggression, they do provide some important correctives to the excesses of a religion of vengeance and hatred. It is not, we recall, in anger that true malignancy lies but in the failure to control the outcome of anger in unthinking violence and in the transformation of anger into a cold and relentless destructiveness. The God who responds to Job with a magnificent description of his power and creativity and who angrily rebukes his comforters for their lack of understanding, is a God whom Job can continue to obey. The truly alien God is the dark assassin, too slippery to be debated with, too hostile to be trusted. Job must find the true God – a God of deep mystery and frightening power, but also a source of creation and order, not chaos and destruction. Perhaps this is the important corrective which a God of anger but not of hatred can bring to the distortions of revelation referred to by Berdyaev. There can be anger in God, but that anger is always part of love and is used for love's creative purposes. When human beings worship and seek to emulate a vengeful God, they make a God in their own unhappy image and they destroy within themselves the imprint of love which God impresses on every creature. Contrary to the imagery of Romans there is no unworthy vessel in the Creator's eyes. All is created in love and destruction comes only from the worship of fake gods.

Heads God Wins – Tails We Lose

In rejecting the idea of a vengeful and wilfully destructive God, we have come close to what could be regarded as the answer of orthodoxy to Job's accusations against God. The fault, if fault there be, can lie only in human failure. Thus Eliphaz brushes aside Job's protestations of innocence: 'Do not think he reproves you because you are pious, that on this count he brings you to trial. No: it is because you are a very wicked man, and your depravity passes all bounds' (Job 22.4–5 NEB). Here we have the moral justification of the evil which befalls us in this life on the grounds that our wrongdoing makes it inevitable that we suffer. Hanson and Dodd use this explanation for the 'wrath of God', but in a way which removes all sense of personal involvement on God's part. 'The wrath' becomes a description of what inevitably happens to those who transgress against the moral order created by God.[10] But to speak of God as being angry or as feeling enmity toward us is, to them, unacceptable anthropomorphism. God merely permits the consequences of our sin to overwhelm us because he will not compromise his commitment to the good. In the light of all that we have seen of the nature of anger, we may well regard such a God as more frightening than an angry God. Here is a God who knows what is happening to us but who does not respond. He sees, from an eternal distance, the destruction of that which he has created, but to be aroused by this sight is for these theologians too 'anthropomorphic'. But is this calm God really the God of the Hebrew prophets or the God of an incarnational theology? Perhaps, of course, these same theologians would not regard it as excessively anthropomorphic to speak of God as 'acquainted with sorrow', failing to see that (as Horatio's description of the ghost in *Hamlet* reminds us – 'A countenance more in sorrow than in anger'[11]) sorrow and anger are two phases of the same reaction to betrayal. It seems a more courageous use of the language which Christian revelation offers us to describe God's reactions in the full range of personal terms borrowed from our knowledge of human relationships, and then to accept the limitations of them all. In so doing we do not pretend that we have any safe, special language about God that will protect us from the error of anthropomorphism.

Following this approach, however, we find ourselves in the world of those theologians who do not hesitate to describe God as angry, because they believe that, faced with human failure, an all-holy God is bound to react with displeasure and to give expression to this displeasure in the form of punishment. Thus Emil Brunner, after describing the enmity of man toward God which has disturbed the created order, asserts,

> there is also enmity on the side of God . . . The Divine Holiness, the unconditional will of God to affirm itself, transforming this disturbance of the divine order into something objective: the necessity for punishment . . . This will is personal. God is present in this anger, it is actually *His* anger. For God is not mocked.[12]

In P. T. Forsyth's classic, *The Work of Christ*, we find an interesting addendum, in which he remarks that he has had second thoughts about his description of the anger of God in the main text (where he rejected the notion of a passion, in favour of the idea of a loving father's discipline). He now feels that he does not want to describe God's anger as though it were 'simply the automatic recoil of His moral order upon the transgressor'.[13] Such a description seems to Forsyth to undercut the idea of God's love, which *must* react because it seeks to save that which is loved. Thus '*both love and anger are real*', for one entails the other, given the presence of sin.

It is beyond the scope of this book to enter into the theories of atonement which writers like Brunner and Forsyth employ in order to show how the enmity between God and humanity is finally overcome so that love triumphs and anger is no more. For our purposes it is sufficient to note that, in this view, God's anger is personal, justified by the failure of humans to obey God, and, were it not averted by Christ's reconciling work, the anger would lead inexorably to eternal punishment in the form of separation from God. Human failure, and human failure alone, accounts for the divine reaction and for the penalty which, but for Christ, would be paid.

But the problem, of course, is that this is not an answer to Job, as the book of Job makes abundantly clear! Job's comforters have failed to answer the problem which is posed, and Eliphaz's argument that Job must have sinned or else he would not have suffered, is blown aside like chaff when God comes in the whirlwind. There is never any suggestion that Job has secret sins. His integrity is fully vindicated, even although he is called upon to repent of his adversarial approach to God (but that, if it was a sin, is subsequent to his suffering in any case). The answer does not lie in the sin-meriting-punishment/ righteousness-meriting-reward formula in which Job's friends take such delight.

Now it is precisely this difficulty which confronts us when we consider arguments in Christian theology which ascribe all earthly misery to human culpability, and thus justify both anger and a tendency to destruction in God. In arguments of this kind, human failure is not demonstrated: it is a necessary assumption of the argument. If one then denies evidence for human culpability in some instances, this is then adduced as further evidence of sinfulness – so lost are we in sin that we are incapable of seeing it ourselves! (At this point the argument is reminiscent of a discussion with the kind of Freudian dogmatism which, knowing our unconscious motivation, takes any denial of it as further proof of how unconscious it is!) As Robert Davidson points out, Job wasn't having any of this rewriting of his life story from his friends: 'The nature of Job's encounter with God was inseparable from his protest against an oversimplistic theology. He refused to allow his friends to rewrite his life to preserve that theology.'[14] One does not have to assert human perfection to question the kind of theology which blames everything on human failure. It is merely necessary to point out that many dreadful things which happen seem to be neither an individual nor a communal responsibility. (We might recall R. D. Laing's description of the little boy dying in agony, quoted in chapter one above.) How then can we be sure that there is any correlation between the evidently terrible things which human beings do to themselves, one another and to the natural world, and the evidently terrible things which happen anyway? We shall hold on to the correlation only if we have a set of basic assumptions which cannot be discarded, namely that (a) it must all be someone's fault; (b) it cannot possibly be God's fault; and therefore (c) even if we cannot see how, it must be humanity's fault either communally or individually. Only within this closed circle can we accept with equanimity that God's anger is always entirely explicable and that, were it not for his love, it would justifiably destroy us.

Beyond Good and Evil

We are left with a third attempt to answer Job, one which accepts that moral justifications for God's actions are not always to be found. This answer appears to be closer to the one which Job is ready to accept, for the one voice to which he listens – the voice of God – gives him no answer to his complaint, but merely demonstrates to him the infinite distance between his understanding of things and the greatness of the creator God. Job repents in dust and ashes, conceding 'I know, God, that you are all-powerful; that you can do everything you want' (Job 42.2 TEV).

James Garrison has interpreted this reaction of Job as follows: 'What Job saw . . . was the numinosity of the Divine itself: a numinosity from which both the evil befalling him and his redemption issued forth – a single continual totality as capable of committing evil as of sustaining the good.'[15] Such an interpretation depends upon a monistic view of God of the type espoused by Carl Jung (in his idea of a quaternity rather than a trinity in the godhead) and by many mystics, Christian and non-Christian. In the difficult thought forms of Jacob Boehme, for example, we have an explanation of the totality of the divine pleroma (of which creation itself is a manifestation of a joy or sport in God), a totality which can encompass good and evil, light and dark, love and anger. All is part of God. God is both light and fire, as the light and the burning flame of the candle are one.

The consequences of this view are potentially destructive of a final confidence in God's benevolence, however. Thus Garrison can write of God's nature as follows:

The God we worship is a terrible God, full of power and might, and as fully capable of manifesting light and darkness as we, God's creatures are. Indeed, if we, the creation of God, made in the divine image, are composed of light and darkness and capable of deeds of great mercy as well as acts of horrible cruelty, why are we so slow in 'allowing' for God the same capabilities we ourselves possess, particularly when throughout our Scriptures we are clearly told that it is a fearful thing to fall into the hands of a living God?[16]

It seems a few short steps from this view of God to James Thomson's cry of unbelief in 'City of the Dreadful Night'

> The world rolls round forever like a mill;
> It grinds out death and life and good and ill,
> It has no purpose, heart or mind or will.[17]

For, if with God we are beyond good and evil, if all is part of his totality, what is it we worship and what do we hope for? This is the central problem with monistic explanations, and Garrison is of course well aware of it. Thus he 'redeems' his account of God by arguing that God (unlike human beings) uses evil only for good: good and evil are not alike to God, but rather the evil is a necessary step to a greater good. The prime example of this is the crucifixion, in which love's purposes are triumphant, only because God, accepting responsibility for evil, puts it to death within himself: 'In Christ, Divinity, wrestling with its own dark side, seeks to experience and at the same time to transcend, the full antinomial tension of opposites in a fully human life.'[18] (This view is strongly reminiscent of Carl Jung's argument in *Answer to Job* that God through the debate with Job and then through the incarnation in Christ learns to overcome his dark side.)

It must be said that Garrison's use of Christology to qualify his monism has the appearance of a convenient escape-hatch from the morally destructive consequences of finding a God who encompasses both evil and good. Alan Watts in *The Two Hands of God* offers a more amusing solution – the 'twinkle in the eye' of God which betrays that the threat of destruction is just 'a celestial version of "chicken"' and that hell is no more than a test of nerve:

In sum, then, the vast metaphysical schism which traditional Christianity proposes is redeemable only if there is a twinkle in the

Father's eye comparable to the 'fear-not' gesture of Shiva in his dance of world-destroying rage. The melodramatic choice between everlasting delight and everlasting torment . . . is a test of nerve.[19]

Although I prefer Watts' version of monism to Garrison's, it appears to me that all explanations of this type strip Christianity and Judaism of their characteristic emphasis on the moral imperatives in human history and the reality of vocation and choice in individual life. Perhaps we could say that they pay too great a price in attempting to give intellectual coherence to our perception that God's anger and God's love are part of the same, trustworthy relationship.

ON LEARNING TO LIVE WITH GOD

Having failed to find a single explanation that accounts for Job's problem with no loose ends, perhaps it is best to accept that coming to terms with the anger of God (and with our anger at God) may not be so very different from our experience of learning to live in close proximity with our fellow human beings. The person of faith (and of the doubt which that entails) knows God not as a theoretical construct to be grasped only with the mind: rather, God, in presence or in absence, is a changing and often puzzling experience, with times of deadness and times of surprising newness. In short, the question of the anger of a loving God is a question to do with the dynamics of a living relationship, the boundaries of which remain uncertain. Thus, still left with something of an enigma, it is perhaps best for us to learn to live with God as best we can, or to give up the attempt as illusory and unproductive. There is nothing new in this. Matthew Arnold's famous lines from 'Dover Beach' seem too simple a contrast between a doubting present and a believing past:

> The sea of Faith
> Was once, too, at the full, and rounded earth's shore
> Lay like the folds of a bright girdle furled.
> But now I only hear
> Its melancholy, long, withdrawing roar
> Retreating, to the breath
> Of the night wind, down the vast edges drear
> And naked shingles of the world.[20]

For what could be more filled with doubt than this ancient lament?

> How much longer will you forget me, Lord?
> For ever?
> How much longer will you hide yourself from me?
> How long must I endure trouble?
> How long will sorrow fill my heart day and night?
> How long will my enemies triumph over me?
>
> Ps. 13.1–2 (TEV)

And this psalm is just one of many (there are over forty) which question God's trustworthiness as plaintively as the case which Job prepares against his divine adversary. In the worship, both communal and individual, of the Jews there is room for debate, for complaint and for pleas to God as well as for affirmations of confidence and praise. Perhaps this element is largely lost in Christian public worship, where we always put on our brightest or our most self-deprecating expressions, but keep our impatience and sense of lostness to ourselves.[21] This is a great loss if we are ever to come to terms with a living God in the midst of a personal and communal life which can shatter our faith in human goodness and take away hope of life itself for us and for our children. What is this defensiveness which will not allow our uncertainties and our distrust of God to intrude upon the calm waters of our worship? What God do we secretly imagine, if we will not challenge him to tell us something of the meaning of a world in which millions starve and millions more devote their financial priorities to weapons of over-destruction? As we consider these questions, we can perhaps realize that our struggles to manage our own anger and to bring something creative out of it are not really at all far removed from our struggles to find and follow a tolerable God, who will really be with us in our darkest moments and whose path is truly a path of peace and not a highway to self-hatred and contempt of others.

The American poet Wallace Stevens, in a poem of disbelief, presents a picture of a 'too, too human God', whom he finds intolerable:

> The fault lies with an over-human God,
> Who by sympathy has made himself a man

And is not to be distinguished when we cry
. . . . .
If only he would not pity us so much,
Weaken our fate, relieve us of woe both great
And small, a constant fellow of destiny

A too, too human God, self-pity's kin
And uncourageous genesis.[22]

Strangely, Christians often act as if they shared Stevens' feelings of distaste, and their 'too, too human God' is therefore kept at a polite distance. Perhaps, indeed, there is a good reason for our hesitancy. The living God *is* more easy to live with if we keep our relationship on a suitably formal footing. To know love is to know fire – and the deeper the love the stronger the fire. We find that in our relationships with fellow human beings intimacy can be painful and that the arousal of strong feelings of mutual attraction and mutual trust carries the obverse, a sense of vulnerability to hurt and anger. The same will be true if we seek truly to know God as a living presence in our lives.

THE GOSPEL OF ANGER

Thus, despite our (sometimes justified) fear of anger, a pastoral ministry which seeks to bring the hope of a living faith to people in distress will struggle to find a creative use of, and a positive response to, anger in ourselves, in others and in God. Anger may be denied, but it cannot be eliminated from human life, and the more we refuse to face up to it the more it will undermine the possibilities of true Christian love through a cloying 'niceness' or an ill-concealed resentment. In considering how we deal with anger pastorally, so that it becomes not an enemy of love, but part of the gospel of love, we must look again at the kinds of situations in which it is most readily aroused, and then consider what a *loving* anger might achieve in overcoming both enmity and apathy. Three aspects of human experience will be considered – vulnerability, loss and oppression – and then a profile of the helper who knows how to use anger creatively will be sketched. Yet this profile, though it may be of some pastoral relevance, cannot possibly provide all the answers to the problems created by anger. An area of mystery will always remain, related to the mystery of love itself. Thus, in a final section I shall recall the 'fire of love' which remains when we look fearlessly at our experience of God and of human life, a fire whose significance – as destructive flame or revealing light – remains uncertain.

Anger and Vulnerability

The closeness of anger to love is most clearly seen in that most obvious of all human characteristics, vulnerability. If we were incapable of being hurt, we would have no need of anger, for nothing could threaten or frustrate us in our imperviousness to pain. But, in fact, human beings can be hurt in many more ways than the risks of injury which they share with other living entities. We possess the fragility of the flowers of the field and the pain response systems of the higher forms of organic life, but in addition our capacity for abstract thought, imagination and complex emotional reactions immeasurably increases the possibilities of frustration and threat in human life. The most painful human experiences are related to the collapse of our aspirations and hopes, to betrayal by those whom we trust, to a loss of any sense of value in our own lives, or to a sense of being discarded, abandoned to our fate, of no concern to any other being. In this spiritual vulnerability, human beings experience the greatest pain, and gain or lose hope and courage most profoundly. (The many stories of heroism and unbroken spirits under appalling conditions of political imprisonment and torture are evidence that for human beings spiritual survival is finally the greatest victory.)[23]

For this reason the anger encountered in pastoral work must not be deplored as selfish or seen as destructive of human value. Very often anger is the struggle of the spirit to survive when a person feels defenceless and betrayed. Anger is at its greatest when it is a cry for love, and the person who suffers silently, stoically, has usually settled for hopelessness. We recall the significance for pastoral care of the 'angry saviour', crying out in Gethsemane and on the cross. (See chapter three above). It is a pagan, not a Christian, ideal which requires rational fortitude in response to the fragile nature of human life and human hopes.

An understanding of the connection between vulnerability

and anger is especially important in pastoral ministry to the sick and the dying. There is an expectation of 'good behaviour' among ill people in which pastoral workers often collude. The 'popular patient'[24] in hospital is cheerful and uncomplaining, showing gratitude to all those helping (especially the professional staff) and always ready to see others as more genuinely ill and in need of help than they. This 'ideal patient' must not show fear, at least not in excess, and outbursts of anger or impatience are seen as inconsiderateness toward the overworked and dedicated family and staff around the sick bed. In such an atmosphere it is not surprising that sick people often find visitors tiring and feel themselves drifting away emotionally from their family. Their struggles to come to terms with their own mortality, with the threats to career or future plans which illness poses, must all be internalized, so that they can put on their best face for their family and other visitors, entertaining them appropriately at the bedside. Ogden Nash captures it well:

> Take the sight of a visitor trying to entertain a patient or a
>   patient trying to entertain a visitor.
> It would bring joy to the heart of the Grand Inquisitor
> The patient either is too ailing to talk or is panting to get
>   back to the chapter where the elderly spinster is just
>   about to reveal to the Inspector that she now thinks she
>   can identify the second voice in that doom-drenched
>   quarrel,
> And the visitor either has never had anything to say to the
>   patient anyway or is wondering how soon it would be
>   all right to depart for Belmont or Santa Anita or Laurel,
> And besides, even if both parties have ordinarily much to
>   discuss and are far from conversational mediocrities,
> Why, the austere surroundings and the lack of ashtrays
>   would stunt a dialogue between Madame de Stael and
>   Socrates.[25]

Ministry to the sick can mediate a 'gospel of anger' to those caught in this social trap of 'good patient' behaviour. This does not mean, of course, insisting that patients express an anger which the helper is convinced they must have (shades of the conversation in the café!). Often the key to anger is to be found in depression and feelings of guilt and foreboding. Patients frequently feel that they must be being punished for wrongdoing, that somehow they deserve their fate and have no right to protest against it. It is thus essential that those who offer pastoral care do not deny the injustice of most misfortune, mediating the God we see in Jesus, as the servant angry alongside us when confronted by the ravages of illness, a fellow ally in the fight against all that destroys human dignity. Like Job, the ill person may need to question, or rail against, God; and this, too, the God we see in Jesus allows, indeed encourages. Those ministers who feel they must defend God against every attack of this kind are revealing their own anxiety about a God who rarely defends himself. They would want a Jesus skilfully rebutting the charges brought against him at his trial, not standing silently before his unjust accusers.

Expression of anger, however, is not itself the means of escape from the three-walled prison in which the sick can find themselves. As we have seen (chapter five above) liberation comes when anger leads to better self-understanding and better communication. Often anger is directed at the wrong targets or smoulders as the kind of bad temperedness which loses the sympathy of others. Effective pastoral care entails helping the suffering person name the enemy directly and identifying what is needed from others to give real help in their struggle. What is it that they fear? Dare they speak of it? And what are the worst aspects of the hurt they experience? – separation from those they love? love of power and influence? a sense of indignity? physical pain and loss of independence? By naming the real enemy, the ill person can move from a sense of helplessness and diffuse anger to a direct and unashamed expression of what they want from others, especially from those closest to them. This is not to deny the anger or to forbid its expression when it wells up within. But it reveals the missing wall of the prison, the way of anger which leads outwards to hope.

Anger and Loss

Even more pervasive than the vulnerability of illness in human life is the universal experience of loss. We experience the pain of loss because part of our natural development is to create attachments to others which sooner or later must be broken.

The series of breaks and changes during the long period of
dependency in infancy creates a pattern which repeats itself
throughout life, in beginning school, in the increased independence of adolescence, in moving home or changing jobs, in
friendships made and broken, in divorce and bereavement, in
retirement and finally in the impending loss of all that is loved
and familiar as death approaches. The irony of the human
situation is that the deeper and more rewarding the attachment,
the more painful the eventual and inevitable loss. Robert Burns
has written lyrically of this conjunction of happiness and
sorrow in love between man and woman, but his words apply
more generally to the human experience of love and loss:

> Had we never lov'd sae kindly,
> Had we never lov'd sae blindly,
> Never met – or never parted –
> We had ne'er been broken-hearted.[26]

Loss and the recovery from loss is perhaps the dominant
theme of the Christian gospel. The famous words of John 3.16
('God so loved the world that he *gave* his only begotten Son'
AV) depicts a loss in God himself which stems from love, a loss
equally described in the hymn of Philippians 2.6–11, describing
the self-emptying of Christ. The story of the life of Jesus is
one of deep attachment and grievous loss. Mother and brethren
are left for the sake of all the disciples and there is no home for
the Son of Man, no permanent resting place for his head, yet
he comes close to others in their homes and at their tables;
the chosen twelve are the companions of Jesus, privy to secrets
and to his vision of what is to come, yet there has to be a last
supper and even then the impending betrayal is known, the cup
of joy mixed with the cup of sorrow; alone in Gethsemane and
abandoned on the cross, Jesus enters the deepest darkness of
the tomb before the new light of resurrection shines on his
grief-stricken family and followers, and illuminates the darkness
of every human loss.

The temptation of piety is to deny the reality of the loss in
the light of the hope which follows. This is a Christianity
without pain, without doubt and despair, which is vacuous
when people have their greatest trials in faith, hope and love. It
is important to remember the lack of tranquility in Jesus when

he faces his testing times. There is little of the Eastern sage, secure in a spiritual detachment, in the reaction of Jesus to the temptations in the wilderness, to the lack of understanding in his disciples, to the religious hypocrisy of his fellow Jews, or to the demands of his heavenly Father, whom he does obey, but in grief and anger. Thus we find in Jesus a real battle between hope and despair, a struggle with which we can identify because it reflects our own reactions to loss, when we will allow ourselves to feel the intensity of the pain without the anodyne of a false religion.

In the bleak times of overwhelming grief, anger may seem just an additional agony. It can be so. Anger, literally in the gut causing nausea and pain, anger bringing clenched fists and tense shoulders, anger causing restless and useless movement, a lashing out at things or a pacing up and down, anger adding hot discomfort and a choking feeling to the wet defencelessness of tears – all these bodily reactions fuel the sense of helplessness and loss of control which grieving often creates. But, like weeping, anger has an important part to play in the healing of the wounds of loss. We have seen already (chapter four above) how the most painful aspect of anger in bereavment is the seemingly shameful anger against the loved person now dead. But such feelings are shameful only when we see anger as inevitably destructive and vindictive. The child is angry with the parent and the parent with the child because each is so close to the other, so easily hurt, so easily comforted and encouraged by bodily closeness with the loved one. Thus the paradigm of loss is loss of the body of the other. (We recall the renewed grief of Mary Magdalene when she finds the tomb empty – 'They have taken away my Lord, and I know where they have laid him,' John 20.13 RSV. Bereavement is at its worst when the body of the deceased cannot be recovered or is so disfigured that it cannot be viewed.) For, it is in bodily presence and bodily absence that the greatest intensity of joy and sorrow are felt. So anger, that disruption of the body created by our perception of frustration or threat, is our most potent appeal for a restoration of that which is lost, our body reacting to a loss of the love which sustains it from cradle to grave.

Once again, then, we may see pastoral ministry as a mediation of a gospel of anger. The greatest danger following

severe loss is the onset of a chronically depressed state in which
the hurt person, unable to endure the pain, settles for a
concealment of the self, withdrawing from the kinds of
experience which could bring fresh losses. In bereavement this
is often achieved by an idealization of the lost relationship,
creating a barrier to any further close involvement with others,
since this would constitute betrayal. In other instances of
unresolved loss early in life, the person avoids all risk in
relationships, using self-effacement and set life routines to
avoid dangerous encounters. Such people often become
increasingly lonely and depressed as the years go on, finding
that their lives have little meaning or sense of direction.
Sensitive pastoral work with such damaged personalities can
help them see that love can be found again when their terror of
self-assertion and especially of the loss of control associated
with anger is overcome. This may require skilled counselling or
psychotherapy, when a distant loss has created a powerful
screen of defensiveness, but sometimes the secret lies more
simply in being a listener who does not share their fear of
negative feelings, who will let them be angry, however
unreasonable that may seem, so that through the recovery of
anger the reality of the lost love can be felt again. Perhaps the
greatest hope in anger is that it is undeniably, unreservedly a
surge of feeling, and for many the greatest hope which a
pastoral helper can bring is the confidence that it is safe for
them to feel again. This for them is the resurrection of the
body, the final hope of the Christian gospel, found here and
now, giving real meaning to eternal life in the mystery of the
world to come.

Anger and Oppression

The anger of the oppressed and anger for the oppressed opens
up a new area of pastoral care, one which the person used to
helping distressed individuals can find confusing and difficult.
Certainly the threats and frustrations which lead to this kind
of anger are clear enough. A potent illustration could be taken
from the impact created by recent television film of starving
children in Ethiopia. The pictures had a horrifying immediacy,
evoking pity and anger in millions of viewers, and so leading to

a dramatic increase in voluntary aid to famine relief agencies. The medium of television made identification with the oppressed possible and so the threat of death by starvation in all its ugliness and injustice was felt by the affluent in Western countries, at least for a time. But the difficulty in using anger effectively in situations of oppression is also illustrated by the Ethiopian example. In the situations of loss and vulnerability which I have already discussed, the anger is directly related to a personal relationship, and the creative use of the anger entails improving that relationship. But in a situation like the Ethopian famine the underlying problem is not in the realm of the personal, but in the political structures which create and sustain the injustices. Thus the personal reaction of affront which leads to dramatic increases in aid can solve the immediate crisis, but it requires changes in government aid policies, in international trade arrangements and in the use of the Third World as a battle-ground for competing political ideologies before the long-term problem of world starvation will be solved. These changes are much harder to achieve than are personal reconciliations, and they appear to involve pastoral ministry in political controversy, in which it is ill-equipped to judge and in which it lacks the power to act.

Yet there are innumerable examples throughout the world of the cries of the oppressed which, if ignored by Christian ministry, reveal no more than the indifference of Churches to the major causes of human suffering. Obvious examples can be found in South America, in the countries of the Communist bloc and in South Africa and other African states with totali-tarian regimes. But equally, in the apparent freedom of Western nations, the rising tide of unemployment, of poverty and of urban violence reveals a social malaise not soluble merely by wel-fare provision. The sacrifice of individuals, or of whole com-munities, to political and economic doctrine creates that mixture of apathy and unrest which periodically flares into seemingly meaningless violence. A Christianity devoted to the increase of love of neighbour and the renunciation of violence cannot avoid creating and responding to anger in the political arena.

Once again the paradigm for a gospel of anger in this aspect of pastoral ministry can be found in the anger of Jesus, as servant and as saviour. Although he never resorted to violence (except in the symbolic act of cleansing the temple) Jesus spoke out fearlessly against the authorities, especially when he was criticized for taking sides with the rejected of society. In his home synagogue he read, and applied to himself, the passage from Isaiah which proclaims good news to the poor, liberty to the captives, freedom to the oppressed (Luke 4.16–21). He would not yield to the authority of Caesar in the things which are God's, and the heat of his anger was reserved for those who thought themselves pious yet neglected justice, mercy and honesty in pursuit of personal gain (Matt. 23.13–28). Although he would gladly have escaped his cruel and painful death, Jesus, the silent one before his accusers, was fearlessly outspoken for the truth that made *him* a prisoner, but set the captives free.

Thus the gospel of anger in the face of political injustice is that we can use our anger to expose falsehood and hypocrisy, reject the compromise that seeks peace at any price, demand the truth, even though to do so means a risk of self, speak honestly about our own uncertainty in the midst of the complex political issues of our day but demand the same honesty from others. The greatest ally of injustice is political apathy, a mentality which leaves in the hands of 'experts' the fate of our fellow humans. When the gospel comes alive in the places where the despised and rejected are to be found, we see with opened eyes what we permit to happen in our name, and in the unsettling experience of anger at oppression we may find the words which are ours to speak, the questions we must ask and the humility to hear for the first time the cry of the oppressed. Thus, in taking seriously the anger of whole groups of our fellow humans, we can learn how the pastoral ministry of truly listening leads to the prophetic ministry of truthfully speaking. For, in the Christian gospel, truth, love and justice are all aspects of the one reality.

Loving Anger

In all that I have said so far about anger in pastoral work an obstacle remains to be overcome. It is the obstacle created by the pastoral helper's own inability to express anger or to cope with experiencing the anger of others. It is common for Christians to feel ashamed of their own anger and to feel unduly threatened by finding that they make others angry. For ordained ministers particularly, there is a subtle pressure to conceal or ignore angry feelings in themselves or others, since such discord seems to discredit the message of peace and love they are commissioned to proclaim. We have seen how this negative evaluation of anger is based on a misunderstanding of its relationship to love. But, while this more positive view of anger may be grasped rationally, it can be much more difficult to accept emotionally and to integrate into one's pastoral ministry. The minister as a quiet and kindly, nice person is such a powerful image that often people may accept the vocation of ministry partly as a means of avoiding the anger they fear within themselves. If this is an element in a person's vocational decision, it means inevitably that being angry 'on duty', as it were, is felt as a major personal failure and the angry pastor's anxiety will be increased by the fear that it may happen again. Not uncommonly, the minister's family are the victims of these outer and inner demands for unremitting niceness. They alone are allowed to experience the 'real' man or woman, but much of the anger they receive has in fact been diverted from its intended target in the church membership or in the pastor's more difficult clients.

Thus ministers of the gospel (and other Christian pastoral workers) are in as much need themselves of that 'gospel of anger' which they try to mediate to others. How can they be angry in a positive way and how can they learn to accept that others can be angry with them? It is probably the physical nature of anger which makes it so productive of anxiety in Christians, since Christianity has had a long battle with a dualism which sees the body as the only focus of sin. To feel one's body responding in anger is to fear a loss of self-control. But such a danger is, as we have seen (chapter two above), far from inevitable and is much more likely the more we fear and deny our anger. Dualism fails to see that body and spirit can equally harm the self and others, and that the body which attacks and destroys is equally the body which comforts and cherishes.

Thus the way to a loving anger in pastoral work is through a more disciplined and less anxious perception of the signals coming from our bodily reactions. By observing the antecedents of anger in ourselves, and by learning to notice similar (though less easily perceived) signs in others, we need no longer be so surprised by surges of anger. (This may at first seem impossible because a well-engrained habit has led us to deny such a reaction, until it simply cannot be ignored.) This improved awareness of the beginnings of anger then gives some space for choice in the way we respond to the other person. Why are we feeling angry? Is it anything to do with them, or are we importing some feelings from elsewhere? If they are the cause, why do they threaten or frustrate us? Can we tell them why we feel angry, honestly and directly?

A frequent experience in pastoral work is simply boredom. People can pour out a catalogue of misfortunes without showing any awareness of how these have arisen or what responsibility they might have themselves for dealing with them. Sometimes the same story is repeated time and again or a crisis, apparently resolved after hours of help, is quickly recreated. Ministers are often adopted by extremely dependent and demanding people, who have run out of 'credit' (as it were) with other helping agencies. A pastoral worker's strong dedication to being helpful and always understanding easily results in a failure to place boundaries on excessive demands of this kind from people. The result is a tedium which can make the helper feel over-used or exploited, yet guilty for such lack of patience.

Yet eventually patience will run out, and the pastor will find ways of avoiding such demanding people or will stop listening with any seriousness to the complaints, thus 'proving' to them, yet again, that nobody loves them. It is the lack of anger on the helper's part which allows such a situation to develop. Why should people not feel annoyed if their time is constantly intruded upon by people who do not wish to change? To be endlessly tolerant of the self-defeating patterns of others is eventually to show a lack of concern for them. Thus feelings of boredom and growing irritation are very important signs that we need to speak more openly and courageously to such people about the effect they are having on us, challenging them to break the pattern and not to use us as another excuse for their lack of hope. It should be a comfort to Christian helpers who feel free to speak in such an honest way that in the ministry of Jesus we see much straight speaking and a refusal to meet every demand upon him, yet always also an accepting love.

Genuine love requires the honesty which anger can provoke.

In a similar way, unhappy people can vent their anger on Christians generally and on ministers in particular, because of their sense of betrayal by others and by God. There is a hopelessness in this kind of anger, because it demands from the other a stereotype which justifies the attack. The helper who is made to feel guilty by the anger of another is quickly caught in the trap of trying to justify God and to prove that piety is different from hypocrisy. But rational argument cannot deal with the unhappiness behind the anger. We cannot relate to another person when the anger they direct at us is not really anything to do with the person we are, but only applies to an image others have of us. Many people avoid receiving help from others by de-personalizing tactics of this kind. A way of love can be found only when people have the courage to resist the illusory world of stereotypes and live in a world of individual differences and uniquely personal pilgrimage. In this real world, the anger of others will still be aroused, but now it will be related to weaknesses and failures which are genuinely ours and therefore are open to us to try to change. This is especially important in the realm of faith and doubt, ultimately the central area for all pastoral work.

In the previous section I wrote of 'learning to live with God', the task which faces everyone who seeks faith in the face of misfortune. We cannot help others in this life task if they insist on making us into graven images of good or evil – the complete hypocrite or the perfect believer. The reality is different. Whether ordained or not ordained, church member or uncertain seeker, all human beings share the same ambiguities in encounter with the living God. It is never the function of pastoral care to pretend that this uncertainty can be avoided. So we must not accept the anger of others if it is directed at an image of the Christian which does not fit our reality. The better anger, the anger which can lead to a companionship side by side on the road to faith, is the anger people express when they realize that we too do not possess certainty and cannot give them the ultimate assurance they demand of us. This is an anger which should learn to accept, even to welcome, realizing that now we – and they – do not fear to feel the fire of love in the realities of human life.

The Fire of Love

In the last of his *Four Quartets*, 'Little Gidding', T. S. Eliot weaves the theme of fire throughout, recalling in numerous ways the Pentecost theme of the Spirit as tongues of fire. In the fourth stanza there is, in a short compass, a wealth of images: the dove of the Spirit, the Phoenix rising from the ashes, the shirt dipped in Nessus' blood (by which Heracles' wife, in seeking to keep his love, caused his agonizing death), the fire of passion and the fire of purification. Throughout the imagery there is the constant theme of love and pain as inseparable aspects of the same reality:

> Who then devised the torment? Love.
> Love is the unfamiliar Name
> Behind the hands that wove
> The intolerable shirt of Flame
> Which human power cannot remove
>   We only live, only suspire
>   Consumed by either fire or fire.[27]

These lines suggest that we look in vain for a comfortable answer to our quest for a wholly coherent pastoral theology of anger. We can see fairly easily how anger goes wrong. We see the false and bloody gods people have created, giving divine sanction to prejudice, greed and pride. We can recognize the sufferings we bring upon ourselves by our preference for niceness, instead of direct communication. We can see our sense of insecurity about the unexplored territory of our own unexpressed anger, and our sense of failure for the times when uncontrolled temper led merely to a destruction of what could have been good. But it is far harder to find a positive way of love which does not fear its fire. How can we dare to move closer to others or to God, if that could cause deeper pain, and we can never be fully sure that we or our God can be trusted? How much risk can we take in the territory that is opened up by our anger and by the anger of God at the oppression of our fellow human beings? Is this to be our fire – that we try, as Christ did, to bring a confrontation that will change the hearts of others? But at what cost?

A pastoral theology which is concerned with human reality in contact with a living God can find no easy answers to these final questions of faith. For this reason, this has not been just a 'how to cope with it' (or indeed a 'how to avoid it') book, with comprehensive guidance for the many pastoral situations in which the anger of others and one's own anger will be experienced, and in which the anger of a loving God will be partly known, but mostly a mystery. To know death and suffering, injustice and sin, is to know the inevitability of anger. But no tidy theological or psychological formula can meet the many choices which then confront us.

Thus I conclude this book by offering the reader no definite ending, only a direction of thought which comes from the closing scene of Archibald McLeish's modern rendering of the story of Job, *J. B.* The dialogue between J. B. and his wife, Sarah, conveys an understanding and a trust of love which goes beyond anger, yet does not deny it:

> J. B.:   The candles in churches are out,
>   The lights have gone out in the sky!
> Sarah: The candles in the churches are out,
>   The lights have gone out in the sky,
>   Blow on the coal of the heart
>   And we'll see by and by . . .
>   we'll see where we are.
>   We'll know. We'll know.
> J. B. (his head falls forward):   – We can never know.
>   He answered me like the . . .
>   stillness of a star
>   That silences us asking . . .
>   No, Sarah, no!
>   We are – and that is all our answer.
>   We are, and what we are can suffer . . .
> (He looks at Sarah and at last sees her).
>   But . . .
>   what suffers, loves . . .[28]

It seems, then, that the deeper we penetrate into the mystery of God, the less we understand rationally why faith endures. We are answered by the 'stillness of a star that silences us asking', and yet, in knowing God in mystery, even in dread and despair, we know our true self as that which suffers and so as that which loves. There was *no* answer to Job – but in his angry questioning he met his God. We could not ask for more from our gospel of anger.

Notes

Preface

1. *Anger – Human and Divine.* Westminster Pastoral Foundation 1982.
2. 'The Anger of a Loving God', *Modern Churchman*, New Series XXV, 3 (1983) pp. 2-11.

Chapter One: God of Anger – God of Love

1. Oscar Wilde, *Selected Poems* (Methuen 1911), p. 4.
2. R. D. Laing, *The Politics of Experience and the Bird of Paradise* (Penguin 1967), pp. 145-6.
3. C. H. Dodd, *The Epistle of Paul to the Romans*, Moffat New Testament Commentary (Hodder & Stoughton 1932), p. 24.
4. ibid., p. 21.
5. ibid., p. 23.
6. A. T. Hanson, *The Wrath of the Lamb* (SPCK 1957), p. 198.
7. 'When God of Old Came Down from Heaven' in *The Methodist Hymn Book* (Methodist Conference Office 1933), No. 276.
8. C. J. Jung, *Answer to Job* (Routledge and Kegan Paul 1954), p. 164.
9. R. C. Zaehner, *Our Savage God* (Collins 1974), p. 242.
10. K. Barth, *Church Dogmatics*, II/1 (T. & T. Clark 1957), p. 368.
11. ibid., p. 363.
12. *idem.*
13. L. Morris, *The Apostolic Preaching of the Cross*, 3rd edn (Tyndale Press 1965), p. 152.
14. R. V. G. Tasker, *The Biblical Doctrine of the Wrath of God* (Tyndale Press 1951), p. 10.
15. See, for example, Morris, op. cit., p. 153; Tasker, op. cit., p. 25.
16. Tasker, op. cit., p. 11.
17. Morris, op. cit., p. 209.
18. A. H. Heschel, *The Prophets* (New York, Harper & Row, 1962), p. 224.
19. R. Haughton, *The Passionate God* (Darton, Longman & Todd 1981), p. 36.

20. Heschel, op. cit., p. 258.
21. J. Donne, *Poetry and Prose* (Oxford University Press 1946), p. 67.
22. Heschel, op. cit., p. 292.
23. J. Moltmann, *The Crucified God* (SCM Press 1974), p. 272.
24. J. Garrison, *The Darkness of God: Theology after Hiroshima* (SCM Press 1982), p. 109.
25. G. Guareschi, *Don Camillo's Dilemma* (Gollancz 1954), pp. 239–42 (edited).
26. I. Howe and R. R. Wisse (eds.), *The Best of Sholom Aleichem* (Weidenfeld & Nicolson 1979), pp. 143–4.
27. M. Luther, *W. A.,* Br. 2, 168.
28. Examples of such useful books are: D. W. Augsburger, *Anger and Assertiveness in Pastoral Care*, Philadelphia, Fortress Press, 1979; D. G. Bagby, *Understanding Anger in the Church*, Nashville, Broadman Press, 1979; S. Southard, *Anger in Love*, Philadelphia, Westminster Press, 1973; A. D. Lester, *Coping with Your Anger: A Christian Guide*, Philadelphia, Westminster Press, 1983. None of these works, however, deals in any detail with the complexity of the biblical and theological material, and there is little discussion of the problem of violence and aggressiveness in human personal and political life.
29. G. Herbert, 'Bitter Sweet' in H. Gardner (ed.), *The Faber Book of Religious Verse* (Faber & Faber 1972), p. 129.

Chapter Two: The Lethal Link

1. A. Roberts and J. Donaldson (eds.), *Works of Lactantius* (T. & T. Clark 1871), p. 7.
2. E. Fromm, *The Anatomy of Human Destructiveness* (Penguin 1977), p. 148.
3. G. Herbert, 'Discipline' in H. Gardner (ed.), *The Faber Book of Religious Verse* (Faber & Faber 1972), p. 131.
4. A. Storr, *Human Aggression* (Penguin 1970), p. 28.
5. C. Tavris, *Anger: The Misunderstood Emotion* (New York, Simon & Schuster, 1982), p. 94.
6. Storr, op. cit., p. 9.
7. Alfred Lord Tennyson, *In Memoriam*, edited by S. Shatto and M. Shaw (Clarendon Press 1982), Canto LVI.
8. S. Freud, *Civilisation and its Discontents*, in J. Strackey (ed.), *Complete Psychological Works*, Vol. 21 (Hogarth Press 1961), p. 111.
9. See Fromm, op. cit., chapter 1.
10. K. Lorenz, *On Aggression* (Methuen 1966), p. 72.

11. S. Freud, *Beyond the Pleasure Principle* in Strackey, op. cit., Vol. 18, p. 62.
12. ibid., p. 38.
13. J. Dollard, *et al., Frustration and Aggression.* Yale University Press 1939.
14. For a full description of the problems briefly summarized here, see A. H. Buss, *The Psychology of Aggression* (Wiley & Sons 1961), chapter 2.
15. Fromm, op. cit., p. 252.
16. ibid., p. 292.
17. R. Frost, 'Fire and Ice' in *Complete Poems* (New York, Holt, 1949), p. 268.
18. Fromm, op. cit., p. 441.
19. See P. E. Mullen, 'The Mental State and States of Mind' in P. Hill and R. Murray (eds.), *Essentials of Postgraduate Psychiatry* (Grune & Stratton 1985), pp. 13–15.
20. No doubt this description sounds too rationalistic for many real incidents of outbursts of anger – consider Don Camillo and the Mayor! But this is the effect of trying to describe something which usually takes place very quickly and with our hardly being aware of it. The point is that aggressive reactions (despite appearances) are not really instinctive in the normal sense of that term: they entail an element of deliberation and choice.
21. Buss, op. cit., p. 89.
22. L. Berkovitz, *Aggression: A Social Psychological Analysis* (New York, McGraw Hill, 1962), p. 207.
23. A. Janov, *The Primal Scream* (Sphere Books 1973), p. 347.
24. Berkovitz, op. cit., p. 212.
25. Tavris, op. cit., pp. 36–7.
26. Matthew 5.21-2. The significance of this saying is discussed in chapter three.
27. B. W. Harrison, 'The Power of Anger in the Work of Love: Christian Ethics for Women and Other Strangers', *Union Seminary Quarterly Review*, 36 Supplement (1981), p. 49. Italics in original.
28. B. Häring, *Embattled Witness: Memories of a Time of War.* Burns & Oates 1976, p. 45.
29. Tavris, op. cit., p. 23.
30. W. B. Yeats, 'The Second Coming', in M. Roberts (ed.), *Faber Book of Modern Verse* (Faber & Faber 1960), p. 73.

Chapter Three: Lover or Demon?

1. G. M. Hopkins, *Poems and Prose*, selected by W. H. Gardner (Penguin 1953), p. 60.
2. 'O brother man', *The Church Hymnary*, 3rd edn (Oxford University Press 1973), No. 460.
3. I am using the terms 'wrath' and 'anger' interchangeably. I do not agree with C. H. Dodd (see chapter one, note 4 above) that 'wrath' has a more impersonal connotation. Indeed, when we wish to indicate a frightening personal anger, wrath is probably the more effective term to use.
4. R. Otto, *The Idea of the Holy* (Oxford University Press 1958–first published 1923), p. 19.
5. P. Volz, *Das Dämonische in Jahwe*. Tübingen, Verlagum Mohr, 1924.
6. W. Eichrodt, *Theology of the Old Testament*, Vol 1 (SCM Press 1961), p. 260.
7. ibid., p. 265.
8. F. Lindström, *God and the Origin of Evil*. Lund, Gleerup, 1983.
9. ibid., p. 241.
10. Some passages in Revelation, e.g. 14.9–11, match in terror those of the Old Testament.
11. A. P. Hayman, 'Rabbinic Judaism and the Problem of Evil', *SJT*, 29 (1976), p. 467.
12. ibid., p. 468.
13. ibid., p. 472.
14. I. Howe and R. R. Wisse (eds.), *The Best of Sholom Aleichem* (Weidenfeld & Nicolson 1979), p. 151.
15. G. B. Caird, *The Revelation of St John the Divine*, Black's New Testament Commentaries (A. & C. Black 1966), p. 92.
16. A. T. Hanson, *The Wrath of the Lamb* (SPCK 1957), p. 170.
17. A. H. Heschel, *The Prophets* (New York, Harper & Row, 1962), p. 226.
18. ibid., p. 5.
19. ibid., p. 289.
20. Francis Thompson, 'The Hound of Heaven' in W. B. Yeats (ed.), *The Oxford Book of Modern Verse 1892–1935* (Oxford University Press 1936), p. 54, 59.
21. W. H. Vanstone, *Love's Endeavour, Love's Expense* (Darton, Longman & Todd 1977), p. 74.
22. James K. Baxter, 'Jerusalem Sonnets', stanza 37, in F. Adcock (ed.), *The Oxford Book of Contemporary New Zealand Poetry* (Oxford University Press 1982), pp. 52–3.

Chapter Four: The Prison of Hostility

1. K. Raine, *A Choice of Blake's Verse* (Faber & Faber 1970), p. 65.
2. W. James, *The Principles of Psychology*. New York, Henry Holt, 1890.
3. L. Madow, *Anger* (Allen & Unwin 1972), p. 72.
4. C. Tavris, *Anger: The Misunderstood Emotion* (New York, Simon & Schuster, 1982), p. 96.
5. ibid., p. 117.
6. A. H. Buss, *The Psychology of Aggression* (Wiley & Sons 1961), chapter twelve.
7. ibid., p. 234.
8. ibid., pp. 238ff.
9. See p. 18 above.
10. A. Storr, *Human Aggression* (Penguin 1970), p. 112.
11. J. Bowlby, *Separation, Anger and Anxiety (Attachment and Loss Vol. 2)*, (The Hogarth Press 1973), pp. 256–7.
12. V. Axline, *Dibs: In Search of Self* (Penguin 1971), pp. 85–6.
13. ibid., p. 112.
14. S. Stephens, *Death Comes Home* (Mowbrays 1972), p. 49.
15. C. S. Lewis, *A Grief Observed* (Faber & Faber 1961), pp. 26–7.
16. ibid., p. 48.
17. E. Kübler-Ross, *On Death & Dying* (Tavistock 1969), p. 50.
18. ibid., p. 67.
19. D. W. Ausburger, *Anger and Assertiveness in Pastoral Care* (Philadelphia, Fortress Press, 1979), p. 8.
20. J. Galt, *Annals of the Parish* (Dent, Everyman's Library, n.d.), pp. 5–6.
21. H. A. Eadie, 'The Helping Personality', *Contact*, 49 (1975), p. 6.
22. F. Nietzsche, *Thus Spoke Zarathustra* (Penguin Classics 1961), p. 82.
23. J. Barke, *The Poems and Songs of Robert Burns* (Collins 1955), p. 202.
24. J. Bagby, *Understanding Anger in the Church* (Nashville, Broadman Press, 1979) p. 34.
25. Buss, op. cit., p. 15.
26. M. Scheler, *The Nature of Sympathy* (Routledge and Kegan Paul 1954), p. 161.
27. See the exposition of Fromm's distinction between benign and malignant aggression in chapter two above.
28. L. MacNeice, 'Brother Fire', in M. Roberts (ed.), *Faber Book of Modern Verse* (Faber & Faber 1960), p. 306.
29. A. Rothenberg, 'On Anger', *Amer. J. Psychiat.*, 128:4 (Oct. 1971), p. 457.

30. *idem.*

31. B. W. Harrison, 'The Power of Anger in the Work of Love: Christian Ethics for Women and Other Strangers', *Union Seminary Quarterly Review*, 36 Supplement (1981), p. 50.

32. R. R. Holt, 'On the Interpersonal and Intrapersonal Consequences of Expressing or Not Expressing Anger', *J. Consultative & Clinical Psychology*, (1970), p. 9.

33. G. Herbert, 'The Church Porch' lines 307–11 in *The Temple, The Country Parson* Classics of Western Spirituality (SPCK 1981), p. 132.

34. Nietzsche, op. cit., p. 83.

Chapter Five: Anger and Liberation

1. Dylan Thomas, 'Do not go gentle into that good night', *The Poems*, edited by D. Jones (Dent & Sons 1971), p. 207.

2. Stevie Smith, 'Anger's Freeing Power', *The Oxford Book of Contemporary Verse 1945–1980* chosen by D. J. Enright (Oxford University 1980), p. 4.

3. Martin Luther King Jr, *Why We Can't Wait* (New York, Signet Books, 1963), p. 80.

4. Stevie Smith, loc. cit.

5. Horace, *Ib,*, I, ii, 62.

6. See the discussion of aggression in chapter two above.

7. R. A. Hoffman, P. M. Kirwin and D. L. Rouzer, 'Facilitating Generalisation in Assertiveness Training', *Psychol. Reports*, 45 (1979), pp. 27–30.

8. B. W. Harrison, 'The Power of Anger in the Work of Love', *Union Seminary Quarterly Review*, 36 Supplement (1981), p. 50.

9. See chapter four above.

10. *Te Hui Oranga*. Duplicated Conference Report, 1984.

11. Dylan Thomas, loc. cit.

12. Ian Crichton Smith, 'Old Woman', *Selected Poems* (Gollancz 1970), p. 15.

13. S. Sassoon, 'Stand To: Good Friday Morning' in *Selected Poems* (Heinemann 1938), p. 27.

14. W. Owen, 'The Soldier's Dream', *The Complete Poems & Fragments* Vol. 1, edited by Jon Stallworthy (Chatto & Windus, The Hogarth Press and Oxford University Press 1983), p. 182.

15. C. S. Lewis, *A Grief Observed* (Faber & Faber 1961) pp. 35–6.

16. Owen, 'The Last Laugh', op. cit., p. 168.

17. Sassoon, op. cit., p. 28.

18. E. Kübler-Ross, *Living with Death and Dying* (Souvenir Press 1982), p. 169.

19. James Matthews & Gladys Thomas, *Cry Rage!* (Johannesburg, Spro-Cas Publications, 1972), p. 9.
20. ibid., p. 12.
21. J. Baldwin, *The Fire Next Time* (Michael Joseph 1963), p. 105.
22. ibid., p. 106.
23. ibid., p. 21.
24. Martin Luther King, op. cit., p. 79.
25. T. D. Hanks, *God So Loved the Third World: The Biblical Vocabulary of Oppression* (Maryknoll, NY, Orbis Books, 1983), p. 115.
26. Matthews, op. cit., p. 3.
27. Baldwin, op. cit., p. 112.

Chapter Six: The Fire of Love

1. J. Boehme, *The Signature of All Things* (James Clarke 1969), p. 214.
2. P. T. Forsyth, *The Work of Christ* (Independent Press 1938), p. 242.
3. T. S. Eliot, 'Four Quartets', *Collected Poems 1909–1962* (Faber & Faber 1974), p. 221.
4. See J. H. Kahn, *Job's Illness: Loss, Grief and Integration* (Pergamon 1975), chapter three.
5. R. G. Collingwood, *The New Leviathan* (Oxford University Press 1942), p. 73.
6. N. Berdyaev, *Freedom and the Spirit* (Geoffrey Bles 1935), p. 92.
7. ibid., p. 93.
8. ibid., p. 175.
9. I. D. Suttie, *The Origins of Love and Hate* (Kegan Paul, Trench, Trubner & Co., 1935), p. 150.
10. See chapter one above.
11. *Hamlet I*, ii.
12. E. Brunner, *The Mediator* (Lutterworth 1934), p. 518.
13. Forsyth, op. cit., p. 239.
14. R. Davidson, *The Courage to Doubt* (SCM Press 1983), p. 183.
15. J. Garrison, *The Darkness of God: Theology after Hiroshima* (SCM Press 1982), p. 168.
16. ibid., p. 162.
17. J. Thomson, 'City of the Dreadful Night', quoted in D. Daiches, *God and the Poets* (Clarendon Press 1984), p. 126.
18. Garrison, op. cit., p. 177.
19. A. Watts, *The Two Hands of God* (Rider & Co. 1963), p. 188.
20. M. Arnold, 'Dover Beach', *Poetical Works* (Macmillan 1890), p. 226.

21. On the omission of psalms of lament from modern hymnaries see Davidson, op. cit., pp. 12–13.
22. Wallace Stevens, 'Esthetique du Mal' from *Collected Poems* (Faber & Faber 1955), p. 315.
23. See V. Frankl, *Man's Search for Meaning.* New York, Washington Square Press, 1963.
24. See F. Stockwell, *The Unpopular Patient.* RCN and National Council of Nurses of the UK 1972.
25. O. Nash, 'Visitors Laugh at Locksmiths or Hospital Doors Haven't Got Locks Anyhow' in *Collected Verse From 1929 On* (Dent 1961), p. 304.
26. 'Ae Fond Kiss' in *Poems and Songs of Robert Burns* edited by J. Barke (Collins 1955), p. 538.
27. T. S. Eliot, loc. cit.
28. A. McLeish, *J. B.* French 1968.

Index

aggression *see* benign aggression, destructive aggression, malignant aggression
anxiety (fear) 19, 29, 38, 52–4, 56–7, 70, 72, 79, 85, 96–7, 103
apathy *see* indifference
Arnold, M. 92, 114
arousal 18–19, 23, 26, 29, 51–3, 57, 62–3, 69–71, 94
assertiveness 72
Augsburger, D. W. 60, 74, 109, 112
Ax, A. 19
Axline, V. 56, 112

Bagby, J. 62, 109, 112
Baldwin, J. 79, 81, 83, 114
Barth, K. 7, 8, 108
Baxter, J. K. 49, 111
benign aggression 23
Berdyaev, N. 85–6, 114
bereavement (grief) 54, 57–9, 62, 76, 97, 100
Berkovitz, L. 110
Blake, W. 50, 112
Boehme, J. 82, 90, 114
Book of Common Prayer 2
boredom 104
Bowlby, J. 56, 112
Brunner, E. 88, 114
Burns, R. 62, 98, 112, 115
Buss, A. H. 26–7, 53–4, 62, 110, 112

Caird, G. B. 42, 111
Cannon, W. B. 18–19, 22
Collingwood, R. G. 84–5, 114
communication 51, 59, 63–5, 67, 71–5, 80–1, 97, 106
covenant 9–10, 42, 45, 81, 85

Davidson, R. 89, 114–15
death 14, 28, 37, 40, 54–5, 57–60, 68, 76–8, 96, 98, 107
death instinct 21–2, 24, 55
depression 53–7, 59, 67, 84, 86, 96–7, 100
destructive aggression: in God 4, 8, 31, 35–43, 48, 86–92; in humans 13, 15, 17, 20–7, 62, 64
divorce 54, 98
Dodd, C. H. 5, 7–8, 10, 87, 108, 111
Dollard, J. 22, 110
Don Camillo 10–13, 82, 109–10
Donne, J. 9, 109
dualism 6, 36, 103

Eadie, H. A. 61, 112
Eichrodt, W. 36, 111
Eliot, T. S. 43, 82, 106, 114–15

faith 32, 34, 48, 61, 67, 77, 79, 86, 92–3, 98, 105, 107
fear *see* anxiety
fight/flight mechanism 18–19, 22
Forsyth, P. T. 82, 88, 114
Frankl, V. 115
Freud, S. 20–2, 52, 55, 64, 86, 89, 109–10
Fromm, E. 17, 23–6, 63, 109–10, 112
Frost, R. 23–4
frustration 21–4, 28, 43, 53, 55, 63, 67, 71, 77, 95, 99–100

Galt, J. 60–1, 112
Gandhi 80
Garrison, J. 9, 90–1, 109, 114
Guareschi, G. 109

guilt 15, 21, 53, 55, 57, 61, 74–5, 85, 104–5

Hanks, T. 80, 114
Hanson, A. T. 5, 7, 43, 87, 108, 111
Häring, B. 30, 82, 110
Harrison, B. 30, 64, 74, 110, 113
hatred 27, 30–1, 56–7, 62–3, 79, 86
Haughton, R. 8, 108
Hayman, A. P. 39, 111
health 14, 18, 29, 51, 53–7
Herbert, G. 16–17, 65, 109, 113
Heschel, A. H. 8–9, 43–5, 108–9, 111
Hoffman, R. A. 72, 113
holiness 4–5, 7–8, 34, 37
Holt, R. R. 64, 72, 113
honesty 13, 33, 71, 81, 84, 102, 104–5
hope 49, 67, 78–9, 95–6, 98–100
Hopkins, G. M. 33, 35, 45, 111
Horace 72, 113
hostility 26, 31, 35, 49–51, 56, 60–2
Howe, I. 109, 111
humour 12–13, 62, 91–2

indifference (apathy) 9, 30, 101
injustice *see* justice
interpretation 17, 22, 25–7, 34, 53–4, 63, 69

James, W. 51, 112
Janov, A. 28, 110
Jesus, anger of 46–8, 67, 95, 97, 99, 101–2
Jung, C. G. 6, 90–1, 108
justice (injustice) 75, 78–81, 97, 107

Kahn, J. H. 84, 114
Keble, J. 5
King, M. L. 66, 79–80, 113–14
Kübler-Ross, E. 59–60, 77, 112–13

Lactantius 17–18
Laing, R. D. 2, 82, 89, 108
Lester, A. D. 109
Lewis, C. S. 59, 76–7, 83, 112–13

life instinct 21
Lindström, F. 36, 111
Lorenz, K. 20–1, 64, 109
loss *see* bereavement
Luther, M. 7, 14–15, 109

McLeish, A. 107, 115
MacNeice, L. 63, 112
Madow, L. 53, 112
malignant aggression 23–4
Matthews, J. 78, 80–1, 83, 114
Moltmann, J. 9, 109
monism 36, 39, 90–2
Morris, L. 7–8, 108
mystery 10, 15, 34, 48, 86, 95, 100, 107
Mullen, P. E. 110

Nash, O. 96, 115
niceness 14, 51, 60, 74–5, 94, 103, 106, 112
Nietzsche, F. 61, 65, 113

Oedipus Complex 21–2
Otto, R. 10, 35, 110
Owen, W. 76, 113

pain *see* suffering
passion 8–10, 24, 47–8, 65, 70, 85, 88, 106
pastoral care 14, 49, 83, 94–105
pastoral theology 32, 106
psychosomatic illness 53–4
punishment 5, 7, 38, 40–3, 58, 72, 85, 88, 96

racial discrimination 78 81
retribution *see* vengeance
'righteous' anger 70
Rothenberg, A. 64, 72, 112

Sassoon, S. 75–7, 83, 113
Scheler, M. 63, 112
Smith, I. C. 75, 82, 113
Smith, S. 66–7, 83, 113
Southard, S. 109
Stephens, S. 58, 112
Stevens, W. 93–4, 115
Stockwell, F. 115

Storr, A.   19, 55, 109, 112
suffering (pain)   2–3, 58, 72, 78–9,
    95, 99, 106–7
Suttie, I. D.   85, 114

Tasker, R. V. G.   7–8, 108
Tavris, C.   19, 31, 53, 109–10, 112
Tennyson, A.   19–20, 109
Tevye the Milkman   13, 40, 82
Thanatos   *see* death instinct
Thomas, D.   67, 75, 113
Thompson, F.   44–5, 111
Thomson, J.   91, 114

Vanstone, W. H.   45, 48, 111
vengeance (retribution)   40–3, 80,
    85–7

violence   *see* destructive aggression
Volz, P.   36, 111
vulnerability   26, 30, 45, 49, 55,
    61–2, 94–7

Watts, A.   91–2, 114
*Westminster Directory of Public Wor-
    ship*   2
Whittier, J. W.   33
Wilde, O.   1, 6, 108
Wisse, R. R.   109, 111
worship   93

Yeats, W. B.   31, 37, 110

Zaehner, R. C.   6, 108